MYSTERY OF MISSING

FLIGHT
F-BELV

MYSTERY OF MISSING FLIGHT F-BELV

STEPHEN WYNN

AIR WORLD

AIR WORLD

MYSTERY OF MISSING FLIGHT F-BELV

First published in Great Britain in 2020 by
Air World
An imprint of
Pen & Sword Books Ltd
Yorkshire – Philadelphia

Copyright © Stephen Wynn, 2020

ISBN 978 1 47384 595 4

A CIP catalogue record for this book is available from the British Library.

Typeset by Aura Technology and Software Services, India.

Printed and bound in England by TJ International.

Pen & Sword Books Limited incorporates the imprints of Atlas, Archaeology,
Aviation, Discovery, Family History, Fiction, History, Maritime, Military, Military
Classics, Politics, Select, Transport, True Crime, Air World, Frontline Publishing, Leo
Cooper, Remember When, Seaforth Publishing, The Praetorian Press, Wharncliffe
Local History, Wharncliffe Transport, Wharncliffe True Crime and White Owl.

For a complete list of Pen & Sword titles please contact

PEN & SWORD BOOKS LIMITED
47 Church Street, Barnsley, South Yorkshire, S70 2AS, England
E-mail: enquiries@pen-and-sword.co.uk
Website: www.pen-and-sword.co.uk

Or
PEN AND SWORD BOOKS
1950 Lawrence Rd, Havertown, PA 19083, USA
E-mail: Uspen-and-sword@casematepublishers.com
Website: www.penandswordbooks.com

Contents

Introduction

Although this book is about the mystery surrounding the loss of flight F-BELV, an aircraft which had been hired by the International Commission for Supervision and Control (ICSC), who were acting in a peacekeeping capacity, it is only right that to put that subsequent loss into context I first provide a potted history of the Vietnam War up until that point in time.

The war actually began on 1 November 1955 and took place throughout Vietnam, Cambodia and Laos. To simplify the war, it was communist-led North Vietnam fighting against the Western-supported government of South Vietnam; but that's where the simplicity stopped. North Vietnam was supported by the Soviet Union, China, and other communist countries from throughout Eastern Europe.

South Vietnam had the backing of the United States of America, South Korea, Australia, the Philippines, Thailand and other anti-communist countries.

In 1961, President John Fitzgerald Kennedy's policy towards South Vietnam was in essence to let the government led by Ngo Dinh Diem defeat the communist-backed rebels, who were trying their best to overthrow them. This was harder than it might have otherwise seemed, due to the ineptness of the South Vietnamese army who collectively did not appear to be up for the fight.

Although the last thing that Kennedy appeared to want was American soldiers on the ground in Vietnam, it was only a matter of time before that became an inevitability. Part of this was due to the inability of the government of South Vietnam to effectively defend themselves and their people from the communist-led North Vietnamese rebels. But it was driven and fuelled by America's almost paranoid state of mind when it came to the fight against the spread of communism.

America had totally misread the situation in Vietnam, and what made matters worse was the fact that they did not appear to have understood the history and culture of its people. This was made abundantly clear when the United States commander in Vietnam, General Paul Harkins, had predicted that there would be an American victory by Christmas 1963. This was the same four-star general who had seen in the beginning of the New Year by having to explain away a defeat by Viet Cong guerrillas at the Battle of Ap Bac on 2 January 1963. Although only three Americans were killed and eight wounded, whilst they lost five helicopters with a further ten being damaged, the South Vietnamese losses were much worse. This led to Harkins being 'slated' in the press back home in America, and his claim about the war being over by December 1963 was shown to be nothing more than words, thrown together to create an unclear picture for the American people. Harkins was replaced as commander of the US forces by General William Westmoreland in June 1964. On his return to America, Harkins retired from the army after having served for thirty-five years which, besides Vietnam, included the Second World War and Korea.

By 1964 the United States had 23,000 troops in Vietnam, but all of that was to change as a result of what has become known as the Gulf of Tonkin incident, which took place on 2 August 1964, when the United States destroyer, the USS *Maddox*, was on a signals intelligence patrol as part of the **De** Haven **S**pecial **O**perations off **T**singat**O** or DESOTO patrols. Such patrols were carried out by United States navy destroyers which were carrying on board what was referred to as a 'mobile van' which was equipment used to gather signals intelligence in enemy or hostile waters.

INTRODUCTION

During that patrol the *Maddox* was attacked by three torpedo boats of the 135th Torpedo Squadron of the North Vietnamese navy. In response the *Maddox* fired three warning shots, but rather than deterring the much smaller but faster torpedo boats, they attacked the *Maddox* with machine-gun fire and torpedoes. By the time the incident was over, one United States aircraft had been damaged, all three of the North Vietnamese torpedo boats had been damaged, four North Vietnamese sailors were killed, with a further six wounded. The United States sustained no deaths or injuries to any of her service personnel. Over the years there has been claim and counter-claim about what actually happened at Tonkin, including who actually fired first. There were also claims and counter-claims of a second incident which allegedly took place on 4 August 1964, but it has been consistently stated by the North Vietnamese that no such incident took place. It has even been claimed that the second incident was manufactured so that the United States would have more reason to immerse herself into the Vietnam conflict.

The result of the incident of 2 August 1964, and the hotly debated one of 4 August 1964, led to the United States Congress passing the Gulf of Tonkin Resolution, which provided President Lyndon B. Johnson with the legal framework to deploy United States troops, which would ultimately lead to the land war in Vietnam.

In a very short period of time the number of American military personnel stationed in Vietnam had risen to 184,000. By the time the fighting finally came to an end in 1975, with the capture of the South Vietnamese capital of Saigon by North Vietnamese forces, the war had exacted an extremely high price in human life, for very little gain of any sense.

In 1965 the number of United States military personnel in South Vietnam increased dramatically, mainly because it was blatantly obvious that the South Vietnamese were losing the war against the communist-dominated Viet Cong, which was in fact a political party in both South Vietnam as well as Cambodia, which actually had its own army in the form of the People's Liberation Armed Forces of South Vietnam (PLAF). The Viet Cong were not at all a 'rag tag' army. They were well drilled, disciplined, very well organised, and boasted both guerrilla units as well as army battalions amongst their ranks.

It became an interesting situation with both the United States and South Vietnam aiming to prevent a communist takeover of the entire Vietnam peninsula, whilst the North Vietnamese and the Viet Cong wanted to unite the two halves of the country, albeit as a communist one.

I still find it somewhat difficult to understand why the United States government, in her almost paranoid state of mind, felt a need to prevent the spread of communism in a country which not only was on the other side of the Pacific Ocean, but was on a different continent more than 8,300 miles away. Why the United States government felt the need to continue the fight for some ten years, in a war which they ultimately lost, and one which cost the lives of some 52,000 young Americans, is difficult to understand. Having said that, in the United States of 1965 the majority of Congress and the nation's people still supported their country's participation in the war. Even though that was the case, protests against the war became more frequent back home in America across the whole country. Many of the demonstrators were either college kids or young men who had previously served in Vietnam and now wanted their nation to pull out of the war. However well-intentioned these young Americans were in their demonstrations against the war, politicians were never simply going to pull out, because there was too much money at stake, as well as the reputations and political careers of certain individuals. There was also the slightly distasteful aspect to be considered which was that there were those who made a lot of money out of the war. It has been estimated that there were more than 2,500,000 men who were deployed to Vietnam at some time during the course of the war.

For each man there would be at least two uniforms issued, two pairs of boots, a helmet, rifle, ammunition, two shirts and a kitbag. So the longer the war continued and the more men who were deployed there, the more money certain individuals would earn.

Besides the fighting on the ground, the United States relied heavily on its offensive air raids on North Vietnam, the first of which was codenamed 'Rolling Thunder' and which lasted from 2 March 1965 to 31 October 1968. It eventually became apparent to the American people that the numbers of enemy personnel its government were claiming had been killed, might possibly not be correct, when North Vietnamese forces launched a co-ordinated national attack against locations all across South Vietnam. Despite the North sustaining heavy casualties, it showed the American people that far from being defeated the North Vietnamese not only remained strong, but had the brains and the manpower to co-ordinate and implement a sophisticated national attack against the somewhat surprised South Vietnamese.

'Vietnamization' was the policy brought in by Richard Nixon's government to finally bring to an end the United States involvement in the Vietnam War. The word came into being during a meeting of the National Security Council on 28 January 1968. The master plan was to teach South Vietnam how to look after its own affairs, principally by being able to defend itself. This included equipping and training South Vietnamese forces, whilst at the same time increasing their use in combat. The flip side of that was the need for fewer Americans to continue the fight against the North Vietnamese, so the quicker the South Vietnamese could be trained, the quicker they could be used in a combat capacity, which meant more American soldiers returning home sooner.

The year 1968 was also the year of the infamous My Lai massacre which took place on 16 March 1968, but it did not become known to the general public until November 1969. How it had been kept secret for so long is staggering in itself, but why is somewhat more obvious. It would not take a genius to calculate the damage which would be caused by the United States' continued presence in Vietnam once news of the atrocity became common knowledge, especially in the eyes of the American public, large numbers being against the war in Vietnam.

The story of My Lai is too lengthy to be included in its entirety in this book in order to do it, and the Vietnamese civilians who were murdered that day by American soldiers, the credit that is so rightly deserved. But it goes to show the complexities of conducting such a war. There are three people who I would like to mention in relation to My Lai, they are three members of a helicopter crew who intervened during the massacre and saved the lives of between twelve and sixteen women and children, including a 4-year-old girl. Those men are Warrant Officer, Hugh Thompson, Jr., a helicopter pilot from B Company (Aero-Scouts), 123rd Aviation Battalion, American Division, crew member Glen Andreotta, who was killed in Vietnam on 8 April 1968, and Lawrence Colburn.

Estimates vary for those killed in the war when it comes down to Vietnamese soldiers and civilians, along with Cambodians and Laotians. Vietnam undoubtedly suffered the most, with estimations varying from around one million to about four million. As for the United States they had 58,220 of their men killed as well as 1,626 who, at the time of writing this book, are still officially recorded as missing in action. Many of these men were probably taken as prisoners of war and never repatriated by the North Vietnamese when the war ended.

During the almost twenty years of the Vietnam War, both the Cambodian and Laotian Civil Wars had taken place. The **Laotian Civil War** took place between 1959 and 1975 and was between the Communist Pathet Lao and the Government of Lao, also referred to as the Royal Lao Government. At this point, I will also make mention of what is now known as the Special Activities Center

(SAC), but was then the **Special Activities Division** (SAD) of the **Central Intelligence Agency** (commonly known as the CIA) who were responsible for covert operations. The division had two units, the Special Operations Group (SOG), who were used for tactical paramilitary operations, and the Political Action Group (PAG), who undertook covert activities related to political influence.

The **Cambodian Civil War** took place between 17 January 1968 and 17 April 1975, and saw the Khmer Rouge, the forces of the Communist Party of Kampuchea (CPK), supported by North Vietnamese forces and the Viet Cong, also known as the National Liberation Front (NLF), pitted against government forces of the Kingdom of Cambodia who, after October 1970, were also supported by the United States and forces from South Vietnam.

Flight F-BELV was an aircraft of the International Commission for Supervision and Control (ICSC) which was lost over Indochina on 18 October 1965. Fifty-four years later, the aircraft involved, a Boeing Model 307 Stratoliner which had been rented by the ICSC from Compagnie Internationale de Transports Civil Aériens in France, is still missing.

In 1955 the Second World War had reached its conclusion just ten years earlier. The Vietnam War would last for almost twenty years, finally coming to an end on 30 April 1975 with the fall of the South Vietnamese capital, Saigon. The United States of America had ended their involvement in the war two years earlier in 1973.

It is due to Sergeant Byrne, one of the passengers on flight F-BELV, that this book is being written as he was my uncle, the younger half-brother of my mother. His story has interested and intrigued me over the years, going back to my school days; I always wondered what really happened. I have my own theory on the matter which you will read about later in the book, as well as an extremely interesting visit I paid to a clairvoyant a few years back.

Chapter 1

Canada's involvement in the Vietnam War

Although not directly connected to the story of flight F-BELV, I believe that this chapter is relevant in providing a fuller picture of Canada's involvement in the Vietnam War, which was much greater than it may have first appeared. Canada did much more than send a few soldiers over as part of a peacekeeping mission, and it is this greater involvement in the war which makes this particular chapter pertinent to the overall story.

Canada was not a belligerent nation during the Vietnam War, although a small number of Canadian soldiers were sent to Indochina as members of the peacekeeping mission, the International Commission for Supervision and Control (ICSC), as well as the much later International Commission of Control and Supervision (ICCS). This was a classic example of, 'if something is not working, change its name ever so slightly, and send it straight back out there to do the same job, and hope that nobody has noticed.'

During the Cold War, which was the period immediately after the end of the Second World War, roughly up until 1989 when the Berlin Wall came down, the North Atlantic Treaty Organization (NATO) came into being, formed in 1949 to combat the spread of communism. Canada was one of its founding members and was instrumental in the forming of that military alliance against the Soviet Union and her allies, who responded by forming their own alliance in 1955, known as the Warsaw Pact.

Canada's 14th Prime Minister was Lester Bowles Pearson, who served in that position between 1963 and 1968 at the height of the Vietnam War. Under his Liberal government Canada managed to stay out of the

Vietnam War, but that had not been a foregone conclusion. Her foreign policy at the time saw her committed to multilateralism and the United Nations, which politically placed Canada in a difficult situation as these two foreign policy objectives clearly clashed with one another.

Canada had been involved in the Korean War of 1950–1953 when, like other NATO countries, she had sent troops to the region in support of South Korea, but as this was undertaken as part of a United Nations resolution it had a legitimacy, which did not infringe upon Canada's policy of opposing illegal acts of international aggression.

Another element which Canada struggled with in relation to becoming embroiled in the Vietnam War was that, being some 7,000 miles away, it was of absolutely no strategic importance to her. In addition to this, Canada did not share America's view on communism in that it had to be actively opposed, even with foreign intervention. Unlike her neighbour the United States, Canada wasn't paranoid when it came to the idea of communism.

On 8 September 1954, the Southeast Asia Treaty Organization (SEATO) came into existence, with its headquarters situated in Bangkok, Thailand. It was Southeast Asia's version of NATO, just a whole lot less effective. Its members were Australia, New Zealand, Pakistan, the Philippines, Thailand, France, United Kingdom and the United States. The countries it was put in place to protect were South Vietnam and Laos, as it was primarily made to block further communist gains in Southeast Asia.

As part of her foreign policy Canada had six prerequisites that would not even allow her to sign up to SEATO, let alone participate in the Vietnam War. These were:

(1) It had to involve cultural and trade ties in addition to a military alliance.
(2) It had to demonstrably meet the will of the people in the countries involved.

(3) Other free Asian states had to support it directly or in principle.

(4) France had to refer the conflict to the United Nations.

(5) Any multilateral action must conform to the United Nations charter.

(6) Any action had to be divorced from all elements of colonialism.

Openly, Canada remained neutral throughout the Vietnam War which as a member of the ICSC, whose job it was to oversee the implementation of the Geneva Accords, she did not really have much choice in, not if she wanted to remain as one of the Commission's nominated delegated members; but behind the scenes, it was an American ally. One of the Canadian delegates who sat on the ICSC was rumoured to have passed messages between the United States and North Vietnam, all of which was done supposedly with the approval of the Canadian government.

This wasn't the only way in which Canada assisted the United States during the Vietnam War. On Wikipedia there is a page entitled, 'Canada and the Vietnam War'; one of the sub-headings of this page is entitled 'Canada's involvement in the War'. It covers how, despite Canada's misgivings in relation to the war and her refusal to become physically involved in it, she still happily exported military supplies and raw materials useful in their manufacture, to the United States. It could be said to be quite shocking that despite her aversion to physically taking part in the war she actually played quite a significant part in it. She happily supplied ammunition, napalm and Agent Orange to the Americans as trade carried on between the countries despite the war.

According to the same article, Canada also supplied the United States Pentagon with aircraft engines and explosives, for use in the Vietnam War. But it did not end there, as Canada also provided beverages, berets, boots, nickel, copper, lead, oil, and brass for shell casings, plate armour, as well as military vehicles. The total of these sales was a staggering $12.5 billion, supplied by an estimated 500 Canadian companies.

So many people were required in Canada to produce all these items that this contributed towards Canadian unemployment figures falling to a record low of 3.9 per cent. Despite all these goods she was selling to the United States and the money she was making from it, Canada wasn't always supportive of her neighbour's tactics in the war. On 2 April 1965, the Canadian prime minister gave a speech at the Temple University in Philadelphia, Pennsylvania, in which he called for a pause in the bombing of North Vietnam, which some Americans, including President Lyndon B. Johnson, thought was a 'bit rich' under the circumstances.

There were even cases where Canadian defence contractors were actually sent to Vietnam to carry out vital repair work on equipment which was used and operated by the United States Army.

Under the Defence Production Sharing Agreement which was a trade agreement signed by both nations in 1956, the Canadian Department of Defence Production (CDDP) and the United States Department of Defense (DoD), tested chemical defoliants together for use in Vietnam. The United States also used Canadian bases and other facilities for weapons testing and training exercises.

There were other aspects of the Vietnam War which also involved Canada in one way, shape or form. These included Canadians who enlisted in and willingly served in the United States military during the war, as well as American 'draft dodgers' and American military deserters, who sought a safe haven in Canada.

In total it is estimated that between 20,000 and 30,000 Canadian men travelled to America and enlisted in the United States military. Of these some 12,000 saw combat in Vietnam, and a total of 110 were either killed in action, died of their wounds or were injured. Another seven Canadians are still officially listed as 'missing in action'.

One of the Canadians who enlisted in the United States Army and went to serve in Vietnam, was Toronto-born Peter Charles Lemon who, at just 19 years of age, was awarded the Medal of Honor, America's highest and most prestigious personal military decoration, which is usually presented by the President of the United States of America. It is on a par with Great Britain's Victoria Cross.

Lemon is the only Canadian-born United States citizen to be presented with the medal as a result of his service in the Vietnam War. At the time of writing this, he was the eighth youngest living recipient of a Medal of Honor, out of seventy-two who were alive at that time.

His award of the Medal of Honor came about as a result of his actions on 1 April 1970 in Tây Ninh Province, in the Southeast region of Vietnam, near the border with Cambodia. The citation for his award reads:

> For conspicuous gallantry and intrepidity in action at the risk of his life above and beyond the call of duty. Sergeant Lemon (then Sp4), Company E, distinguished himself while serving as an assistant machine gunner during the defense of Fire Support Base Illingworth. When the base came under heavy enemy attack, Sergeant Lemon engaged a numerically superior enemy with machine gun and rifle fire from his defensive position until both weapons malfunctioned. He then used hand grenades to fend off the intensified enemy attack launched in his direction. After eliminating all but 1 of the enemy soldiers in the immediate vicinity, he pursued and disposed of the remaining soldier in hand-to-hand combat. Despite fragment wounds from an exploding grenade, Sergeant Lemon regained his position, carried a more seriously wounded comrade to an aid station, and, as he returned,

was wounded a second time by enemy fire. Disregarding his personal injuries, he moved to his position through a hail of small arms and grenade fire. Sergeant Lemon immediately realized that the defensive sector was in danger of being overrun by the enemy and unhesitatingly assaulted the enemy soldiers by throwing hand grenades and engaging in hand-to-hand combat. He was wounded yet a third time, but his determined efforts successfully drove the enemy from the position. Securing an operable machine gun, Sergeant Lemon stood atop an embankment fully exposed to enemy fire, and placed effective fire upon the enemy until he collapsed from his multiple wounds and exhaustion. After regaining consciousness at the aid station, he refused medical evacuation until his more seriously wounded comrades had been evacuated. Sergeant Lemon's gallantry and extraordinary heroism, are in keeping with the highest traditions of the military service and reflect great credit on him, his unit, and the U.S. Army.

Sergeant Lemon's actions on 1 April 1970 were truly remarkable, but for someone who was still only 19 years of age they showed outstanding bravery of the highest order which, it could be said, would not usually be expected of one so young. His bravery that day really did belie his tender years.

Many young American men who did not wish to join their country's military and go to serve in Vietnam chose to dodge the draft, hence the term 'draft dodgers', and instead sought refuge in neighbouring Canada. As might be imagined this caused a lot of controversy, especially amongst those young Americans who wished to immigrate to Canada. Many of them were stopped at the border and prevented from entering Canada unless they could prove that they had been discharged from their American military service. American draft dodgers and military deserters had sought refuge in Canada since 1965, and in those early days, before restrictions were placed upon them, they were treated as immigrants rather than being classified as refugees.

On 22 May 1969, this approach by the Canadian government changed. They announced that immigration officials would not and could not ask American citizens about their military status if they sought permanent residence in Canada at one of their border posts with the United States. The exact number of those young Americans who entered Canada as a deserter from the American military or as a draft dodger is not known, but there were tens of thousands.

It is an interesting fact that on 21 January 1977, on his first full day in office, the American President Jimmy Carter granted unconditional pardons to the many thousands of draft dodgers who, having left the country during the Vietnam War, were now returning to the United States, and to those who had chosen to remain in Canada.

Canada was also the country to which many American military deserters headed. Some had already served in Vietnam and had no desire to return there, whilst others had been called up and were still undergoing their basic training, deciding that involvement in the Vietnam War was not for them. Unlike the draft dodgers, there has never been a pardon for any of them.

Michael Shaffer had served in the American army for six months in the late 1960s, when he applied for conscientious objector status. His application was denied and instead he was informed that he would be going to Vietnam, but he refused to draw his rifle and was ordered to be court-martialled. On Labour Day in 1970, which is traditionally on the first Monday in September each year, he managed to escape to Canada where he remained for the next five years. In 1975, and as a direct result of President Ford's clemency programme, Shaffer went to Fort Dix in New Jersey to hand himself in, seeking the 'undesirable discharge' that had been promised to deserters like Shaffer, who handed themselves in to American authorities. Despite the clemency having been offered by none other than the president of the United States of America, the United States Army decided that he wasn't entitled to it. Instead he was informed that court martial proceedings against him would be resumed. Although initially detained he was released after some legal intervention. It then took a further two years before a federal court ordered the United States Army to provide Shaffer with an honourable discharge as a conscientious objector.

One way or another, Canada played an extensive role in the Vietnam War and although much of it wasn't on the battlefields of Indochina, a large part of what they did do was significantly undertaken in the background.

Chapter 2

North Vietnamese soldiers

In comparison to the might of the United States military which they were up against, the North Vietnamese and Viet Cong were poorly equipped and greatly under-resourced, but they had the advantage of fighting in their own backyard. They literally knew the terrain that they were fighting in like the back of their hand and they used that knowledge to their advantage.

It could never be called a conventional war because one belligerent was a powerful, well trained, disciplined force – who knew or understood little of jungle warfare – whilst the other was, in reality, a guerrilla army. There were very few occasions where both sides faced each other across a battlefield. It could be argued that the North Vietnamese and the Viet Cong actually had an advantage over the American soldiers and marines, as Vietnam already had the experience of fighting against a major Western power, in the form of a French army during the First Indochina War of 1946 to 1954. A war which ultimately resulted in France having to withdraw her formidable forces. Many of those from France who fought against the North Vietnamese were elite soldiers and included the riverine forces, which were France's Commandos Marine. To add to their numbers they also utilised the French Foreign Legion who were, and still are, a formidable fighting force. Most of these men were not French, many being Germans who had fought during the Second World War, either with the *Wehrmacht* or the Waffen-SS. There were also a number of Spaniards who had fled to France after the end of the

Spanish Civil War in 1939. Some of these men enrolled in the Legion for financial reasons as work of any kind was hard to find in the years immediately following the end of the Second World War. For others it was a simple case of having enjoyed the camaraderie which came with their wartime experiences, rather than the fighting and killing.

If anything, it could be said that the fighting men of France were far more formidable than those which America had to offer. The French forces of 1946–1954 were in the main experienced battle-hardened veterans who were fighting out of choice, whereas the vast majority of American soldiers were inexperienced young men who didn't want to be there. The majority of young Americans who ended up in Vietnam did so because they had been conscripted and therefore had no choice in the matter. For most it was a case of seeing out their time, usually a twelve month tour, and then getting back home hopefully still in one piece.

For the North Vietnamese and Viet Cong, they were fighting for their nation's liberty. These were young men who were both idealistic and communist who had seen their homeland governed by other countries for more years than they could remember and they had had enough. They wanted their country back. They wanted to free their country and its people from what they perceived to be a form of latter-day slavery.

Whereas part of the American strategy for the war was to bring it to a conclusion as quickly as possible, the North Vietnamese were happy for it to grind on until they were victorious. The leadership in Hanoi knew from their experience against the French that the longer the war continued the better their chance of winning it, uniting the country and ridding it once and for all of its American aggressor. They knew that the Americans were incurring a great cost by being involved in the Vietnam War, and that the more forces they sent the higher the financial cost would be to them. Hanoi knew that politically the Americans only had a small window of opportunity to win the war in Vietnam before public opinion would turn against them and want their troops out. More importantly, they knew that this would be the case each time an American soldier was killed and sent back home in a body bag inside a coffin. In politics allies quickly become enemies, especially if they feel that they are going to be on the losing side or that their powerful positions are under threat. Moreover, they knew that the American public would tire of the war long before their politicians would. No matter how politicians try to ignore public opinion, they will have to listen eventually; but unfortunately politics is just a game, life and death are not.

The North Vietnamese certainly had the dogged determination to see it through to the bitter end. They had everything to win and absolutely nothing to lose. The Viet Cong were trained by the North Vietnamese, to cause trouble in South Vietnam. Their training included the use of weapons, explosives, tactics and hours spent in the 'classroom' being reminded of the history of their situation, almost an indoctrination of what they were fighting for.

Chapter 3

CIA involvement in the Vietnam War

It was not my intention in this chapter to write a complete history of the CIA's involvement in Vietnam, but just to give a flavour of what they did leading up to and including October 1965, and the disappearance of flight F-BELV. Also exploring how that involvement could be connected to the way in which the North Vietnamese, Pathet Lao and Viet Cong conducted themselves as a result.

The Central Intelligence Agency, or CIA, the acronym by which it is more commonly known, had operatives working in Indochina, Southeast Asia and Vietnam as early as 1954. This was a delicate time for the region as despite Vietnam having been given independence after the end of the Second World War, it remained under French rule until 1954, when they finally left. The problem was that with France leaving, the nation was at the beginning of a new journey. America's position in the matter wasn't helped by the fact that she was paranoid, having an inherent fear and loathing of communism becoming the new way forward, and of it spreading throughout Southeast Asia. America saw it as her personal duty to prevent the spread of communism. Although that view was more readily understood in her own backyard, as she was after all 'the land of the free', why she became embroiled in a war thousands of miles away across the Pacific Ocean, on another continent, is unclear. It is still hard to believe that her involvement in Vietnam was solely to prevent the spread of communism.

However, this wasn't just about communism, it was also about money and lots of it. Countries such as America and Great Britain had many profitable business interests in the region. The fear was that communism would be seen by the people as the new way forward for the whole of Southeast Asia, costing Britain and America millions in lost investments, a situation which undoubtedly would not sit easily with either nation.

One of the problems with the CIA's involvement in Indochina was that boundaries became blurred. There was a very thin line between political reasoning and criminality in what they were doing, which led to the obvious question of who was in charge. Was it the president of the United States, American politicians or the actual CIA? There was most definitely an element of having no checks in place to monitor their actions, which could have been down to working in a political vacuum where the maxim had become, 'don't bother us with the detail, just get the job done no matter what it takes', against, 'this is what they want us to do, this is how we will do it'.

The CIA and the individuals who worked for them were undoubtedly patriotic and believed that their actions were carried out with the best of intentions, but sometimes no matter what they did, things did not get any easier for them. One example of this would be the capture of Viet Cong, especially if such events had come about as a result of a CIA operation or involvement. For some reason the South Vietnamese government decided that they would treat captured Viet Cong as criminals rather than prisoners of war, this meant that they would be put before the courts, receive a short prison sentence and then be released, free to return to being a Viet Cong fighter once again. With the benefit of hindsight and the application of common sense, that really does sound like a crazy idea.

During the time of the Vietnam War the CIA came up with Operation Chaos, but this wasn't something which took place in the jungles of Vietnam, Laos or Cambodia, but on the streets of the United States. What made it even more staggering was that it was authorised by the then President, Lyndon B. Johnson, to be later expanded under President Nixon. He gave his permission for the CIA to spy on American citizens, with their main task being to infiltrate student organisations who were behind many of the nationwide anti-war demonstrations which had taken place. The reason for the operation was to try to establish if there were any sinister foreign influences behind the demonstrations and if so, was any of it communist related. Once a group such as for example, the Black Panther Party (or 'Black Panthers'), a black-nationalism movement and civil rights group, had been targeted, the plan would be to get CIA operatives to try to subvert the group from within.

Operation Chaos highlighted the main problem with the CIA. They were given a direction by the president of the United States which somehow led to them targeting women's groups, such as Women Strike for Peace (WSP, or Women for Peace). This peace activist group was founded in 1961 by American lawyer Bella Abzug, and Dagmar Wilson, who was an American anti-nuclear testing activist, and an illustrator of children's books. The domestic spying aspect of Operation Chaos expanded further when the CIA targeted the Israeli Embassy in Washington, and Jewish groups who were involved in nothing more sinister than combating anti-Semitism, and uniting people of the Jewish faith.

By the time Operation Chaos was finally terminated in 1974, the CIA held files on 7,200 Americans, and a computer index totalling 300,000 civilians and approximately 1,000 groups. These are figures which are genuinely shocking and far beyond the remit of what they had been tasked to do. News of Operation Chaos finally became public in December 1974, when a report appeared in the *New York Times* claiming that the CIA had conducted illegal domestic activities, including secret drug testing, during the 1960s. The commission issued a report in 1975, which touched upon certain CIA abuses including mail opening, wiretapping, and surveillance of domestic dissident groups, which would have been directly connected to Operation Chaos. This led directly to President Gerald Ford establishing the President's Commission on CIA Activities within the United States, to look at the CIA's actions throughout the 1960s. The commission was led by the Vice President, Nelson Rockefeller, and is sometimes referred to as the Rockefeller Commission.

Chapter 4

Disappearance of Flight F-BELV

Flight F-BELV disappeared on a routine flight between Vientiane, in Laos, and Hanoi, on 18 October 1965. The aircraft concerned was carrying nine members of the International Commission for Supervision and Control (ICSC). At the time of its disappearance the aircraft was carrying a total of thirteen people on board. The four crew members were all French citizens. Of the nine ICSC members there were: five of the Indian delegation; one representative from Poland; and three members of the Canadian delegation. Two of these were from the Hanoi office and the third person, Sergeant James Sylvester Byrne, was from the Saigon office.

Flight F-BELV, a Boeing 307 Stratoliner four-engine aircraft, was on a routine flight from Wattay Airport, Vientiane, which is the capital of Laos. The aircraft, with thirteen passengers and crew on board, departed Wattay at 1505 hours on Monday, 18 October 1965, and was making its way to Gia Lam Airport, in Hanoi, North Vietnam, a journey which should have taken one hour and fifty-three minutes. The aircraft was owned by the Paris, France, based company, Compagnie Internationale de Transports Civil Aériens (CITCA), and was on contract to the ICSC. The flight's captain, Henri Domerque, confirmed the departure of his aircraft with the control tower at Vientiane.

Just fifteen minutes into the flight at 1520 hours, Captain Domerque radioed ahead to the control tower at Gia Lam Airport, confirming that he had departed Vientiane at 1505 hours. He also confirmed his

16

flight path for the rest of the journey which showed that he would be over Muong Xen in North Vietnam at 1555 hours and Phu Ly, North Vietnam at 1644 hours, with his anticipated arrival in Hanoi being at 1658 hours. The authorities at Gia Lam Airport confirmed that they had received the information of flight F-BELV and cleared it for arrival in Hanoi. When the aircraft did not arrive at its scheduled time the authorities at Gia Lam Airport made repeated attempts to make contact with F-BELV, but there was no response, making the radio message from Captain Domerque at 1520 hours the last known contact anyone had with him.

When F-BELV failed to arrive in Hanoi, the airport authorities at Gia Lam simply assumed that it had returned to Vientiane, despite not having received any such message from F-BELV that this was the case. Why the authorities at Gia Lam Airport did not make contact with the airport at Wattay to confirm whether F-BELV had in fact returned to Vientiane, is not known.

At 1815 hours the same day the ICSC office in Hanoi sent a message to its counterpart in Vientiane explaining that flight F-BELV would not be able to land at Hanoi, but that clearance had been obtained for it to do so at 0900 hours the following morning.

The ICSC office in Vientiane were, as might be expected, somewhat confused by that message and replied to their colleagues in Hanoi asking for clarification of their previous message. At the same time they confirmed that F-BELV had departed Vientiane on time at 1505 hours and had been expected to arrive in Hanoi at just before 1700 hours. They also confirmed that the aircraft had not returned to Vientiane. The message ended with a request for confirmation that F-BELV would arrive back in Vientiane at 0900 hours on Tuesday, 19 October as scheduled. Although this message was prepared at 2240 hours on Monday, 18 October 1965 and marked as 'operational immediate', it was not actually sent until 0720 hours the following morning. The delay was due to ionospheric interference.

Sometime after receiving this message the ICSC office in Hanoi re-sent its message from the previous day, but corrected it to show that it should have read that flight F-BELV 'did not land' rather than it had been 'unable to land'. The Hanoi office was now even more confused. Having not received a reply to the message they had sent at 1815 hours the previous day, until 0720 hours on Tuesday, 19 October, they had spent the previous thirteen hours believing that F-BELV had in fact returned to Vientiane, whilst the office in Vientiane had spent the same period of time believing it was on the ground in Hanoi.

To make matters worse, the ICSC office in Vientiane had not been aware of the delay in the transmission of its message of 2240 hours from the previous day until mid-morning on 19 October. Realising that there was now a problem they sent a 'flash message' to their colleagues at both the Hanoi and Saigon offices, at 1035 hours, requesting an immediate investigation. It was now some nineteen hours since anything had been heard from flight F-BELV, meaning that valuable time had been lost.

By the late morning of 19 October 1965, it was clear to all concerned that there was a problem with flight F-BELV. It had only been at 0758 hours that same morning that the authorities at Gia Lam Airport had thought it prudent to contact their counterparts at Saigon airport to inform them that flight F-BELV had not arrived in Hanoi and that they had assumed it had returned to Vientiane.

It can be appreciated that hindsight is a wonderful thing, but it wasn't until sometime in the afternoon of 19 October 1965, and then only after a number of communications between the ICSC offices in Vientiane, Saigon and Hanoi, that they came to the somewhat obvious conclusion that flight F-BELV was missing. It was at this time that the ICSC officials requested detailed information from the North Vietnamese authorities concerning the last radio contact that the control tower at Gia Lam Airport had with F-BELV, and what its position was at that time. In addition they also requested permission to conduct an air search along the air corridor between Vientiane and Hanoi. The confusion over the whereabouts of flight F-BELV lasted for over sixteen hours, add to this the additional time it took to secure permission from both Laos and North Vietnam to be allowed to conduct an aerial search, and it was than twenty-four hours after flight F-BELV had left Vientiane before the first search aircraft was in the air.

It has to be remembered that a search such as this would be a very delicate situation to manage, as on the ground there was a civil war going on in Laos and of course there was the war in Vietnam. There was the added consideration that the North Vietnamese authorities might have concerns that a search conducted by an agency from a foreign country could also be used for other purposes, even though the ICSC were in the region as a peacekeeping organisation and not as an ally of the Americans.

Flight F-BELV actually began its journey in Saigon, having left there at 1130 hours on 18 October, although its original departure time had been at 0900 hours, but it was delayed. Its first stop was in Phnom Penh, Cambodia, before arriving in Vientiane at 1300 hours, which was the time it had originally been due to leave there. Its departure was then put back to 1500 hours and it ended up departing five minutes later than scheduled.

The flight plan which had been filed in Saigon showed that the route from Vientiane would take the aircraft direct to Hanoi via Muong Xen (19'23"N 104'E) and Phu Ly (20'33"N 105'55"E), North Vietnam. The flight plan also showed that the altitude the aircraft would be flying at would be 3,600 metres, or 11,811 feet, at an airspeed of 165 knots.

If F-BELV had made it to Hanoi that would have been its final leg of the day's journey. It would have then remained there overnight and begun the return journey the following morning.

The thirteen people on board were:

Henri Domerque	Pilot	France
Camille Lemee	Radio Officer	France
Marcel Ropers	Flight Engineer	France
Albert Gustin	Steward	France
Captain C.K. Bhattacharjee		Indian Delegation
Lieutenant Bhola Singh		Indian Delegation
S.L. Bhalla		Indian Delegation
J. Prasad		Indian Delegation
M.R. Ramani		Indian Delegation
Mr Meluch		Polish Delegation
Sergeant James Sylvester Byrne		Canadian Delegation
Corporal Vernon J. Perkin		Canadian Delegation
John Douglas Turner		Canadian Delegation

Out of all those on board flight F-BELV here is a more detailed look at the three Canadian personnel:

John Douglas Turner was from Vancouver, and was the Canadian Permanent Representative on the ICSC.

Corporal Vernon J. Perkin of the Royal Canadian Hussars was from Regina, and was on his way to Hanoi to take up guard duty at the office of the Canadian Delegation.

Sergeant James Sylvester Byrne of the Royal Canadian Army Service Corps, from Aylmer, was attached to the Canadian Delegation in Saigon and was making the trip to Hanoi as a courier.

The ICSC Bureau in Hanoi officially informed the North Vietnamese authorities at noon on Tuesday, 19 October 1965, that flight F-BELV had failed to return to Vientiane. In response the North Vietnamese authorities requested information about the flight.

On **19 October 1965**, the Secretary General of the ICSC in Laos sent an urgent message to the acting Foreign Minister of Laos, requesting that he assign aircraft of the Royal Laotian Government to help in the search for F-BELV.

The representative of the political wing of the Laotian People's Liberation Army, the Neo Lao Hak Sat, more commonly referred to as the Pathet Lao, was also contacted and asked that permission be granted for search aircraft to be allowed to fly over Pathet Lao territory on both 19 and 20 October.

A headquarters for the search and rescue operations was established at the Canadian delegation at Vientiane, in the offices of the International Commission for Supervision and Control. Another office was set up at Wattay Airport, Vientiane, whose role was to brief and debrief all air crews involved in the search.

The first aircraft to leave Wattay Airport in Vientiane, Laos, to begin the search for F-BELV, did so at 1500 hours on 19 October. This was a Boeing 307 Stratoliner of the Compagnie Internationale de Transports Civil Aériens. It had the call sign F-BELU and it conducted a search between Vientiane and the Laotian border with North Vietnam. To have gone any further without the agreement and knowledge of the North Vietnamese authorities would have risked any such aircraft being shot down. The search lasted for three hours before F-BELU returned to Wattay Airport. Later that afternoon, two helicopters, which were able to fly at a much lower altitude, also conducted a search along the same air corridor for 103 minutes, but once again no trace of flight F-BELV was discovered.

On **20 October** the search was drastically ramped up with a total of twenty-one aircraft involved in the search. This included two Stratoliners of the Compagnie Internationale de Transports Civil Aériens, which were F-BELX and F-BELU, two helicopters from the ICSC, nine aircraft from the Royal Laotian Air Force, five aircraft from Air America and Continental Air Services, who were active in the area under contract to the United States Agency for International Development, one from the RAF, along with two more aircraft

21

from Mission Militaire Française. The combined search time was 120 hours and covered an area up to 7 miles each side of the known flight path of F-BELV, from Vientiane to the Laos, North Vietnam border, although none of the aircraft flew over territory which was occupied by the Pathet Lao, as at the time of the search permission had not been given.

The search operation to locate F-BELV continued up until 16 November 1965, although it was the three days between 20 and 22 October 1965 when it was the most focused. After that, the searches continued but were more sporadic. Towards the end of the search time, activities were restricted to the confirmation of reported sightings of aircraft wreckage. Four sightings were reported, two of which turned out to be false. The other two were identified as being the wreckage of a C-46 and a C-47, but nothing was found of the wreckage of F-BELV.

Added to these searches, the North Vietnamese informed the ICSC from time to time about searches which they had apparently carried out along the notified flight plan of F-BELV from the border with Laos all the way to Hanoi, but there was never any cheering news.

The reality of the situation was that when it came to North Vietnam, or territory controlled by the Pathet Lao in Laos, there was no way of knowing what if any searches had actually been carried out. It would be fair to say that there was mistrust on both sides.

The last radio contact from F-BELV was at 1520 hours when Captain Domerque contacted the control tower at Gia Lam Airport in Hanoi, at which time the aircraft would have been travelling at 165 nautical miles per hour or 3.1 nautical miles per minute, this meant that between 1505 hours, when F-BELV had departed from Vientiane, and the last radio contact at 1520 hours, it had travelled a total 46.5 nautical miles. At the time the Pathet Lao forces controlled large swathes of the North and East of the country, so it would appear that although it is not known how long after the last radio transmission flight F-BELV was actually lost, there is a more than fair chance it was in territory under the control of the Pathet Lao; but that in itself is the problem. The aircraft could have come down immediately after that last radio transmission, or at any time during the next thirty-five minutes, which means that it could have travelled for another 100 miles.

The following is a 'Confidential' message sent on **3 November 1965** from the Canadian Army Headquarters in Ottawa to Saigon, possibly to the Canadian delegation of the ICSC, but it isn't clear who the main recipient was. It was also sent to the Canadian Embassy in Paris. It reads as follows

Commission Report on Missing Aircraft

We are in constant touch with the families of missing Canadians. Many of them continue to believe that the aircraft (flight F-BELV) will be found with passengers alive and well. While we for our part continue to hope also, we think it is now necessary to initiate preparations against the eventuality that there will be no actual reported survivors.

As mentioned previously, the report of our Ad-Hoc Committee could, in those circumstances, be useful for legal purposes. It could form the basis for instance of certificates of presumption of death in the event that the aircraft is not located or, although located, bodies are either not found or cannot be identified. As you know these certificates are legally necessary for admin of estates, settlement of life insurance policies, and payment of death benefits. They are not issued except on rather conclusive proof of death.

We should hope that the report would therefore contain full description of flight; all available information about its disappearance; record of search measures taken; outline of search measures which could not be taken and why; and analysis of all possible reasons for aircraft's disappearance.

If aircraft is located, report should also describe its condition. If not located, report should analyse geographical, climatic and political considerations governing possibility of finding it within reasonable period, possibility of reaching it and likelihood of passengers having survived in those circumstances.

Report should also include list of passengers, together with a statement that Commission (or at least Canadian) personnel were on duty and not considered responsible for disappearance of aircraft. If bodies are located the report should identify them, if possible. It would also be helpful to have certificates of death from competent local authorities, if these are obtainable.

Unless there are reasons to the contrary, or difficulties of which we are not aware, it might be useful to have the report adopted as official commission document at formal meeting.

Please let us know whether you foresee difficulties in the preparation of this report and what sort of timetable you anticipate for its preparation and final conclusion.

The above could certainly be taken as a direct attempt at trying to influence the content of the ICSC's Ad-Hoc Committee's report, taking into account that the committee had already been given a mandate of what aspects of the aircraft's disappearance they should be looking for. Having said that, it appears on the strength of the content of this memo that the Canadian authorities had already accepted that even if flight F-BELV was ever located, then all of those who had been on board the aircraft, would be dead. It appears that they were acting in the best interests of the missing Canadians, to secure the best possible insurance payout for their immediate families.

On **18 October 1966**, exactly one year to the day that flight F-BELV disappeared, a confidential message was authorised by Mr C. Hardy who worked in some kind of government capacity in Ottawa. The message was originated by a Mr J.H. Taylor, and was addressed to 'Saigon' and the 'Paris Embassy' and was entitled 'Insurance Claims':

> You were right to have obtained assurance from secretariat, that claims can be processed directly rather than through them. As long ago as last February (your letter 62 of Feb 19) you recommended processing claims in Paris. Indians at that time had enlisted assistance of Indian Embassy in Paris; first approach to quai was made after consultation between Indian and Canadian Embassies.
>
> Since then our Embassy has been frequently in touch with quai. These enquiries have yet to produce settlement; on the other hand, we have been kept informed of why there have been delays and how long these may last.
>
> Our interest is in obtaining fair settlement for missing Canadians as quickly as possible. We have formal assurances that the two year rule would not be binding to the extent that delays were attributable to French administrative processes. Perhaps there is no way in which these could have been materially reduced. At the same time, we have the impression, perhaps unfairly, that we would have been no better off and perhaps even worse off had we entrusted follow up to secretariat. Certainly what indications we have had of degree of secretariat interest in Saigon and Indian Embassy involvement in Paris suggest a routine bureaucratic approach.

This is why we would rather stick to processing these claims ourselves. At the same time we will be glad to keep you, and through you, secretariat, informed where we stand.

Our letter of May 20 contained a detailed description of documents submitted on behalf of Turner and discuss extent to which this documentation would satisfy requirements of French law and regulations. You say your files show no sign of further action. This must mean your copy of our letter of May 31, has gone astray, it would appear.

Albeit an incident which occurred nearly ten years after the disappearance of flight F-BELV, mention could be made here regarding the destruction of an Air Vietnam DC-4 aircraft, by an anti-aircraft missile fired from North Vietnam, as it made its way from the Laotian capital of Vientiane en route to Saigon, shortly after taking off. Once again there was no known reason for the attack.

Chapter 5

Weaponry of the Pathet Lao and North Vietnamese

One aspect concerning the disappearance of flight F-BELV which has to be considered, is the type of weaponry available to the Pathet Lao and North Vietnamese forces at the time.

One thing is certain, regardless of what happened to the missing ICSC aircraft, it was lost over either Laos or North Vietnam. It left Vientiane in Laos and never reached its destination in Hanoi, North Vietnam.

Beginning with the Pathet Lao, they controlled areas in the north and east of Laos, and when they were formed in 1956 as an official political party their stated goals were to fight on the side of the communist cause to rid their nation of Capitalism, Western Colonialism and Imperialism.

On 18 October 1965, part of the flight path of F-BELV would have taken it through eastern parts of Laos, this was an area which also consisted of a large number of North Vietnamese forces. Both the Pathet Lao and the North Vietnamese had a plethora of weaponry at their disposal.

The **Pathet Lao** had three different types of anti-aircraft guns. These were the **ZPU-4 5mm** quadruple anti-aircraft autocannon, which were Russian built. It first came into production way back in 1949 and is still in use today, but the development of the gun began at the end of the Second World War in 1945. All the weapons in the ZPU range have air-cooled quick-change barrels, allowing them to fire a variation of different ammunition at a rate of some 150 rounds per minute.

The quad barrel ZPU-4 was usually used from a four-wheeled carriage. When it is in the firing position it is lowered onto firing jacks. It had the added advantage that it could be easily moved around to different firing locations in a short period of time, which made it a very useful piece of defensive equipment to have as part of an armoury.

It was capable of hitting a target flying at an altitude of up to 5,000 metres, but was accurate and effective up to about 1,500 metres.

The **M1939 (61-K)** 37mm gun is another weapon from the Russian armoury in use by the Pathet Lao. Having been developed during the early stages of the Second World War, it became a useful addition to the Russian anti-aircraft capability. It proved its worth on the Eastern Front, and during the war this gun was responsible for bringing down a staggering 14,657 mainly German aircraft.

It had an altitude range of 6,700 metres, but it was accurate and effective up to about 3,000 metres, and required a crew of eight men.

The **AZP S-60** 57mm gun was yet another Russian piece of armoury. It was easily transportable and had a firing base on four wheels which could be lifted off the ground and secured on brackets to give the weapon more stability. It was a very effective weapon, but only up to around 1,500 metres in altitude.

As for the **North Vietnamese Army** (NVA), they were known to have had Russian-made self-propelled anti-aircraft guns from at least the end of December 1964, and by February 1965 they had more than 2,000 such weapons. They also had gun batteries which included the **ZPU-1/2/4**, single, double and quad, 14.5 mm anti-aircraft machine guns, very similar to those which the Pathet Lao forces possessed. The **ZU-23** twin 23mm anti-aircraft twin-barrelled autocannon. It was developed by the Russians in the late 1950s and had been specifically designed to engage low-flying aircraft or helicopters at a range of just over a mile. It was such an impressive weapon that 140,000 of them were produced.

The ZU-23 was usually carried on the back of a small two-wheeled trailer, which was easily converted into a static mount.

The description of the M1939 37mm anti-aircraft gun is included in the previous section on the anti-aircraft weaponry that was available to Laos forces. The AZP S-60 57mm anti-aircraft gun is the same as that used by the Laotian forces. The 85mm air-defence gun **M1944** was yet another piece of Russia-made anti-aircraft equipment that the North Vietnamese were fortunate enough to acquire. They were a very useful weapons system to have and were subsequently organised into anti-aircraft regiments, which were then turned into divisions. The M1944 version had a longer barrel and fired a much more powerful round.

The **KS-19** 100mm air-defence gun was yet another weapon to come out of Russia; a weapon they had developed and first brought into action just after the end of the Second World War. It was a towed weapon carried on a four-wheeled trailer, giving it high mobility at short notice, although it did require quite a heavy vehicle to tow it as well as a fifteen-man crew. Only one round could be loaded at a time, but an experienced crew were more than capable of firing off fifteen rounds per minute. Despite being an anti-aircraft gun it was also used as a ground weapon, especially against armoured targets.

Another weapon, the **S-75 Dvina**, was in essence a Soviet-designed surface-to-air missile, first used in 1957 and still in use today. The first aircraft to be brought down by one of these missiles was on 7 October 1959, when one was used to shoot down a Taiwanese Martin RB-57D Canberra, which was a specialised high-altitude reconnaissance aircraft. It was actually hit by three such missiles whilst flying at a height 65,600 feet. At the time, the credit for bringing the aircraft down went to a Chinese fighter aircraft in an effort to keep the S-75 programme a secret. This same weapon was also responsible for bringing down the U-2 spyplane which American pilot Francis Gary Powers was flying through Soviet airspace on 1 May 1960.

It is worth noting at this point that throughout the Vietnam War, the North Vietnamese extensively used the S-75 missile in the protection of Hanoi. During the war the North Vietnamese had a total of ninety-five S-75 systems, with more than 7,600 missiles to go with them, of which 6,806 were fired. The United States lost a total of 3,374 combat aircraft during the war, of which the North Vietnamese claim 1,046 were shot down by the use of S-75 anti-aircraft missiles.

If an aircraft was struck by one of these, especially in the front section, the chances are the crew would not have had any chance to send out a distress signal. It would also follow that any such stricken aircraft would have been blown to pieces in the sky, well before it landed on the ground below.

The **S-125 Neva** was a Soviet-designed high-altitude surface-to-air missile defence system. It first came into service in 1961 and is still in use today. It has a shorter effective range than other similar types of surface-to-air missile and can engage targets that are flying at a much lower altitude. It is also designed to travel at a much slower speed. Being a more up-to-date weapon, it is more readily able to deal with electronic counter-measures than the S-75 model was.

One curious point regarding accounts of the searches carried out on 19, 20 and 21 October 1965, and considering reports which put the tree canopy level at 100 feet in height, is that if flight F-BELV had crashed through the tree tops there would surely have been a gap indicating where it had fallen. No such evidence was ever discovered, which points very strongly to the possibility that it was struck by an S-75 missile and disintegrated in the sky. If that is what happened then the question has to be 'Why?'

One of the aircraft that the North Vietnamese had to call upon was the **Cessna A-37 Dragonfly**. It was actually an American, light attack aircraft. It first came into service in 1964 during the Vietnam War. It is not clear how it came to be in the possession of the North Vietnamese. They also had three different types of MiG jets, the 17, 19, and 21, all of which were Russian made.

The single-seat **MiG-17** first came into service on 14 January 1950, but didn't see combat until 1958 in what was known as the Second

Taiwan Strait Crisis, which was a conflict between the Republic of China (ROC) and the People's Republic of China (PRC).

The **MiG-19** was a single-seat, twin-engine fighter aircraft, which was the first aircraft from the Soviet Union to be capable of supersonic speeds. The year 1965 saw a MiG-19 bring down an American aircraft in combat for the first time. The aircraft in question was a Lockheed F-104 Starfighter supersonic interceptor. The pilot of the aircraft, Captain Philip E. Smith, ejected from the stricken aircraft and was captured by the North Vietnamese. He spent eight years in captivity, before being released on 15 March 1973.

The **MiG-21** was a supersonic jet fighter, which first flew on 14 February 1956 and is still in service with some nations today. It remains the most produced supersonic jet in aviation history. It is hard to believe that we live in a day and age of ever changing technology, yet an aircraft that is 60 years old remains one of the best in the world.

The timing of the appearance of these weapons was no coincidence, as February 1965 was also the time when the United States began bombing North Vietnam, day and night, with the number of raids increasing in their intensity as the year continued. The North Vietnamese also had fifteen different types of aircraft at their disposal, including Chinese MiG jet fighters

The North Vietnamese and the Americans had to continually change tactics to outwit each other. In the early part of 1965, rather than place anti-aircraft units at strategic locations to specifically defend a particular installation, they would spread out in a line across the known flight path of incoming American bombers. This in turn led to the Americans changing their bombing tactics, which then led to the North Vietnamese deploying their anti-aircraft weapons in a different way, and so it went on, with the Americans trying to establish a more effective bombing strategy whilst the North Vietnamese continued to come up with better defensive tactics to give themselves the best chance of shooting down American aircraft.

Part of the revised American tactics included their aircraft flying at altitudes no lower than 4,500 metres, which is interesting when taking into account that flight F-BELV had filed a flight plan, on her ill-fated journey from Vientiane to Hanoi, which included a flight level of only 3,600 metres.

Chapter 6

The Model 307 Stratoliner

Although considered by many to be a reliable 'workhorse' of an aircraft, the Boeing aircraft company built just ten Model 307 Stratoliners, between 1939–1940. Of these, five of the aircraft were purchased by the Paris based Compagnie Internationale de Transports Civil Aériens, mainly to fulfil contract obligations they had in place with the ICSC, to carry out regular courier runs between the several ICSC offices located throughout Indochina: Phnom Penh in Cambodia, Saigon in South Vietnam, Vientiane in Laos, and Hanoi in North Vietnam. The original Model 307 Stratoliners could carry just thirty-three passengers, but those which were used by the ICSC, in Indochina, had been adapted to cater for as many as sixty passengers.

The 307 Stratoliner was somewhat ahead of its time, being both one of the first four-engine transport aircraft to be produced during the early years of the Second World War, whilst also being the first pressurised commercial aircraft. The only reason many more of them weren't built was due to the war, when Boeing factories were adapted to produce much needed military aircraft for the United States Army Air Force (USAAF) war effort.

It is worth considering that by the time flight F-BELV disappeared, the aircraft was already 25 years old.

The remaining five of these aircraft had been used by the Air Transport Command of the United States Air Force unit during the Second World War, and were re-designated as C-75s. By the early 1960s, the 307 Stratoliners were still considered to be both dependable and durable.

During the years that the aircraft were used in Indochina by CITCA, three were kept fully operational at all times, whilst a fourth would be undergoing thorough maintenance checks, ensuring that all of CITCA's Stratoliners were airworthy. Following the loss of F-BELV, it was reported by the ICSC that they had thoroughly checked the airworthiness of all the aircraft under their control and found them to be in perfect working order, each holding a valid certificate issued by the French government to prove this.

In 1968, the *Boeing* magazine carried an article by a captain who worked for Air America, and who was familiar with the Stratoliner, having flown it many times. The article read:

> 307s are a pleasure to our eyes over here. They are being well kept. After discussing the aircraft with the head of the CITCA maintenance department and some of the mechanics, it became very obvious that all of the people involved in the work on, and the flying of, the planes are highly impressed with the old beauties appearance, which is spotless, highly finished paint work, which is always fresh. Their interiors are clean and neat. The cockpits look like new, all of the equipment is present and accounted for. It is most interesting to see the face of a disbelieving young fighter pilot as the 307s trundle out and take gracefully to the air among supersonic F-4s and new Boeing 707s.

Not all of those who worked for the ICSC who travelled on the Stratoliners on a regular basis, would have necessarily agreed with the words proffered by the Air America captain. But it could not be argued that the aircraft of CITCA were not very well maintained, on a regular basis, which made it unlikely that flight F-BELV was lost due to mechanical failure. This is supported to a large degree by the fact that no distress signal was ever received from the crew of the aircraft.

An official Canadian report some three years later painted a somewhat different picture of the aircraft:

> Various aspects of the air service, such as the structural integrity of the aircraft, suitability of the installed navigation/communication equipment, proficiency of crews and air traffic control problems have been considered. Recent incidents, particularly while operating in North Vietnamese airspace, have prompted a closer look from a safer angle.
>
> The aircraft, though obsolescent (becoming obsolete – passing out of use), have an unlimited service life providing maintenance schedules are met. It is understood that all aircraft are kept serviceable but only two are used to provide service at any one time.
>
> From all reports there is no concrete evidence which would indicate that the aircraft are not airworthy. However, the performance limitations and outdated navigation/communication equipment are such that it can be stated categorically, that a more modern aircraft and related equipment is most desirable.

The report which was written more than two years after the loss of flight F-BELV, in January 1968, also included numerous issues which were relative to the flights between Vientiane and Hanoi, that some might feel were germane when flight F-BELV was lost. The report continued:

> Following the incidents on 5 May 1967 and 27 October 1967, the lack of positive control, in a controllable

situation, became evident. The critical portion of the flight is between the North Vietnamese border with Laos, and Hanoi due to the air activity in North Vietnamese air space and particularly in the Gia Lam terminal area. The initiative to minimize the risk to the International Commission for Supervision and Control aircraft, and of course personnel, was taken by the ICSC following the 5 May 1967 incident then followed up by civil and military controlling authorities in Saigon at the urging of the United States Embassy. It should be noted, however, that this action is on the part of the United States airborne forces only and regardless of how effective these measures are, a real element of risk due to the action of other forces, still remains.

The report also included remarks and observations concerning what was believed to be the vulnerability of the Stratoliner aircraft:

Because of the limited speed and altitude capability of the Stratoliner, it is vulnerable to airborne as well as ground based North Vietnamese defensive forces. As it must operate in the lower levels over mountainous terrain, flight following with ground based radar is effective for only approximately 50 nautical miles, north east of Vientiane. The radar units involved are very busy and at best can only provide service in an emergency. It follows that an aircraft with a greater speed and altitude range would reduce risk, firstly by shortening the flight time in North Vietnamese airspace and therefore, exposure; secondly, by cruising at higher altitudes, say at 15-18,000 feet, radar tracking would be greatly improved; and thirdly, the risk of a hit from ground fire would be minimal.

This aspect of the report is rather confusing; why should there be an issue around the vulnerability of Stratoliner aircraft employed to move personnel of the ICSC around Indochina, when the aircraft travelled along authorised and pre-used flight paths which all parties on the ground were aware of? This included knowing the times that the flights would be travelling at and how long each stage of the journey would take. It doesn't seem to make sense to talk about replacing the Stratoliners, stating that they were vulnerable to ground attack, when they were moving around in a controlled and agreed environment.

This argument is strengthened further when considering the fact that the crew were all civilian personnel. There is absolutely no way that they would have agreed to fly over areas where they were likely to be fired at by military ground forces of any kind. Add to this the fact that the ICSC would never place their own personnel, or those who they were dependent upon to move them around Indochina, in danger by allowing them to fly over areas without official permission, or over territory potentially vulnerable to anti-aircraft fire.

Captain Domerque and his crew were all experienced individuals and had flown the Saigon to Hanoi route on many occasions. Under the circumstances, it is difficult to even contemplate that human error by any member of the crew played any part in the disappearance of flight F-BELV.

In relation to any possible weather factors being connected to the loss of F-BELV, all known reports from the time and day in question strongly suggest that this is not the case. A copy of the weather map provided to the crew of F-BELV, before they departed from Saigon at the beginning of their journey, included reports of scattered cumulus and altocumulus clouds over most parts of Indochina. It also included information regarding the general weather conditions they could expect to encounter at different points along the route between Vientiane and Hanoi. In addition to this, the North Vietnamese authorities advised the ICSC office in Hanoi, that on 18 October weather conditions were good along the corridor of the flight path taken by flight F-BELV over the territory of North Vietnam, which included the Gia Lam Airport, at the time of the flight.

The agreed minimum altitude for F-BELV to fly at throughout its journey was 3,600 metres, which should have taken it to approximately 1,000 feet above the highest point along the entire route. The terrain was extremely rugged along the corridor that F-BELV was flying, ranging from deep valleys to steeply rising peaks. Two in particular were notably high. One of them standing at 2,711 metres, was Mount Xai Lai Leng, in Laos, which was right by the border of North Vietnam, just south of the flight path corridor. Another peak along the route stood at 2,452 metres, so was not quite as high, but still something to contend with.

Besides the continuous hostilities which had been taking place for several years between the forces of the Royal Lao Government and the communist-backed fighters of the Pathet Lao, the Ho Chi Minh Trail also ran from the North Vietnamese and Laotian border, before winding its way through Laos to South Vietnam.

Not only were fighting factions on the ground a potential threat, the air force of the Royal Lao Government supported by aircraft from USAAF were also prominent in the area, although at the time of flight F-BELV there were no such attacks or raids taking place and nothing unusual in the way of air traffic.

It would have been abundantly clear, even to fighting units on the ground in Laos, that F-BELV was not a military aircraft and as such posed no direct threat to them by way of either machine guns or bombs, as it was incapable of delivering such payloads.

Operation Rolling Thunder had begun in North Vietnam in March 1965, with USAAF attacking military targets across the country, and whilst there were breaks in the bombing raids, they were frequent and intense with many of them centred on and around Hanoi and the major nearby port of Haiphong.

On 18 October 1965 there was activity in North Vietnam involving United States bomber aircraft which meant that defensive ground forces, of which there were many, were on full alert, but despite this it would still have been difficult to mistake the ICSC aircraft as an enemy bomber.

On 22 October 1965 a very strange incident took place, when the United States authorities took the somewhat unusual decision of informing the Canadian delegation to the ICSC in Vientiane, Laos, that no USAAF aircraft had been involved in the loss of flight F-BELV. This immediately raised suspicions that the opposite was true.

A sense of what life was like for those who had to endure a journey on board one of the CITCA courier flights into the potential powder keg that was North Vietnam, appeared in a 1967 edition of *Life* magazine. An American photojournalist and writer, Lee Lockwood, wrote a piece about a journey he took to Hanoi on board one of CITCA's Stratoliner aircraft. Part of Lockwood's report confirmed just how regular the flight that F-BELV took was for the ICSC.

> At Phnom Penh, the capital of Cambodia, I picked up the International Control Commission plane, which flies every Friday and every other Tuesday to Hanoi. The ICC plane, piloted by three French men was an ancient four-engine Boeing 307. We let down en route at Vientiane, Laos. The plane had to leave from here and arrive in Hanoi, exactly on schedule, flying within a 20 mile corridor. Clearance for any deviation in flight plan, must be obtained several days in advance, from the North Vietnamese, the United States Air Force, the United States Navy, the Royal Laotian military and the commands of the Pathet Lao guerrilla forces, any of which is likely to open fire on any stray airplanes.

Chapter 7

International Commission for Supervision and Control

The International Commission for Supervision and Control (ICSC) was first established in July 1954 with the purpose of ending hostilities in Indochina, and in doing so, creating the conditions for France to safely withdraw her troops from the region, large swathes of which she had for so long been in control of.

The Commission was set up as a result of the Geneva Conference on Indochina that same year, which had been co-chaired by the USSR and the United Kingdom. The conference started just two weeks after the end of the Battle of Dien Bien Phu, which took place between 13 March and 7 May 1954. The battle had been an attempt by the French Far East Expeditionary Corps, a colonial force of the French Union Army, to draw out the Vietnamese Viet Minh communist revolutionaries and deliver them a devastating and final defeat, by the use of superior fire power. Unfortunately for the French their plan failed. In fact they suffered such a heavy and unexpected defeat that the First Indochina War ended soon afterwards on 21 July 1954, and with it France's involvement in Indochina. This resulted in the Geneva Peace Accords, one each for Vietnam, Laos and Cambodia.

The agreement resulted in a ceasefire between the French and the Viet Minh, with both sides having to regroup either side of an implemented de-militarised zone which was put in place along the 17th Parallel. This in effect separated the country into two parts, North Vietnam and South Vietnam, which is how it remained until the end of the war in 1975. The final outcome of the conference was not universally liked and actually resulted in South Vietnam dissociating itself from it, with no nation being willing or prepared to sign it. Maybe this was because the conference's final declaration called for the subsequent elections to be held under the supervision of the ICSC.

Historically, it is interesting to note that what was, after all, an attempt to end the conflict in Indochina actually resulted in prolonging it for the next twenty years.

The Commission only had three member delegations, Canada, India and Poland, with India presiding. Its mandate was the not so easy task of supervising the ceasefire between the warring factions. Intentionally or otherwise this also provided all sides of the conflict. The headquarters of the ICSC was set up in Hanoi on 11 August 1954, with what were known as observer teams set up in different locations throughout Indochina, including what had become North and South Vietnam. Four years later on 31 March 1958, the headquarters were moved to Saigon, but the office in Hanoi was kept on as a Commission outpost.

Looking back on the years of the Vietnam War, the question has to be asked what if anything did the ICSC actually achieve. It is a question which most people would have no answer for. Along the way they undoubtedly worked hard and had committed people working for them, who achieved a few victories especially in the early years, but nothing really substantial. One of the factors behind this was the political aspect of the situation. To a large extent they were relatively powerless to impose rules or regulations on the factions involved. It could be said that they were somewhat a 'toothless tiger', with world politics more readily determining what happened in the region. As the situation worsened throughout the region, it wasn't helped any when Russia, China and the United States all became involved. In the case of the first two it was in a supporting role rather than a more direct one such as that which America had chosen, as she did her utmost to try to stem the flow of communism throughout the world.

In many respects the ICSC presented as a non-entity, as though it was established in order that those at the Geneva Conference of 1954 could feel good about themselves, that they achieved something positive. It is worth noting that, despite the fact the Conference was co-chaired by the United Kingdom and the USSR, neither were part of the ICSC, which in turn begs the question how was it decided upon that Canada, India and Poland would be the three countries who would be on the ground carrying out the day-to-day work of the Commission.

The Second World War had seen the best part of six years of fighting throughout Europe and North Africa, in an effort to defeat the madness of Adolf Hitler, during which time Emperor Hirohito had sought dominance throughout the Far East and the Pacific.

Then there had been the Korean War 1949–1953, and the First Indochina War 1946–1954. Between the end of the Second World War in 1945 and the end of the Vietnam War in 1975, there had been another fifty-five wars, uprisings or armed conflicts. In essence, the fighting had never stopped. It was as if the end of the Second World War was a signal worldwide for all downtrodden nations to break free from Colonial-type masters or power-mad dictators.

It seems that the Geneva Conference of 1954 could be perceived as nations making positive efforts to intervene in such a conflict, but for any such intervention to succeed, it had to have the backing, support and a real desire by these nations to make it work.

Below is a list of the wars, conflicts and uprisings, as alluded to above.

Chilean Military Coup	1973 - 1973
Yom Kippur War	1973 - 1973
Guinea-Bissau War of Independence	1963 - 1974
Laotian Civil War	1959 - 1975
Rebellion and genocide in Burundi	1972 - 1972

First Sudanese Civil War	1963 - 1972
Bangladesh Liberation War	1971 - 1971
Indo-Pakistan War	1964 - 1971
Israel v Egypt	1969 - 1970
Nigerian Civil War	1967 - 1970
North Yemen Civil War	1962 - 1970
First Kurdish - Iraqi War	1961 - 1970
Football War - Honduras v El Salvador	1969 - 1969
The Six-Day War	1967 - 1967
Dominican Republic Coup	1965 - 1965
Congo Crisis	1960 - 1965
First Rwandan Civil War	1963 - 1964
Vietnam Civil War	1955 - 1964
Sino-Indian War	1962 - 1962
Rwandan Social Revolution	1959 - 1962
Algerian War of Independence	1954 - 1962
Bizerte Crisis	1961 - 1961
Bamileke War	1955 - 1960
Cuban Revolution	1953 - 1959
Darul Islam Rebellion	1953 - 1961
Mosul Uprising, Iraq	1959 - 1959
Cameroon War of Independence	1957 - 1959
Tibetan Uprising	1956 - 1959
Lebanon Crisis	1958 - 1958
La Violencia	1948 - 1958
Malayan Civil War	1948 - 1960
Soviet Invasion of Hungary	1956 - 1956
Sinai War	1956 - 1956
Mau-Mau Uprising	1952 - 1960
Tunisian War of Independence	1953 - 1956
Moroccan War of Independence	1953 - 1956
First Taiwan Strait Crisis	1954 - 1955

Hukbalahap Rebellion	1946 - 1954
First Indochina War	1946 - 1954
Korean War	1949 - 1953
Bolivian Revolution	1952 - 1952
Soviet Union v Baltic Partisans (Forest Brethren)	1945 - 1951
Third Sino-Tibetan War	1950 - 1950
Arab-Israeli War	1948 - 1948
Jeju Uprising	1948 - 1949
Greek Civil War	1946 - 1949
Chinese Civil War	1946 - 1949
Costa Rican Civil War	1948 - 1948
First Kashmir War	1947 - 1948
Alwaziri Coup	1948 - 1948
Indian Partition Communal Violence	1947 - 1948
Civil War in Mandatory Palestine	1947 - 1948
Telangana Rebellion and Indo-Hyderabad War	1947 - 1948
Paraguayan Civil War	1947 - 1947
Madagascar Rebellion	1947 - 1948
Taiwan Uprising	1947 - 1947

After the Commission came into being, it had some 1,400 staff. Of these 1,086 were from India, with Canada and Poland providing 160 members each. By the time the Commission was disbanded as a result of the Paris Peace Accords in 1973, the total strength of those still attached to it was just 300. Maybe this was a reflection of the Commission's lack of ability to be an effective organisation.

In some respects the Paris Agreement signed on 27 January 1973, which officially ended the war in Vietnam, brought with it some unintended comedy. The signing of the Paris Agreement brought the International Commission for Supervision and Control to an end, only to be replaced by the brand new, International Commission of Control and Supervision. It is possible that the ICSC was never really disbanded;

perhaps the powers that be simply threw the words of the title into the air, and they all came down again in a slightly different order.

The new Commission's mandate was to supervise the ceasefire, oversee the withdrawal of United States and Allied forces from the area, as well as the repatriation of all captured military and civilian personnel, from all sides. Canada and Poland remained as members of the new Commission, but India had had enough, and withdrew, whilst Hungary and Indonesia became new members. Canada was also feeling the pressure after nearly twenty years and, although still a member of the new Commission, she only agreed to remain in that capacity for a period of sixty days. This actually continued until the end of July 1973, before Canada withdrew her service altogether. This wasn't an action which she took lightly, but was a result of years of frustration with the Commission's shortcomings.

It could be said that Canada's inclusion as part of the International Commission for Supervision and Control was not necessarily a good fit for her, as politically she had declared her recognition of South Vietnam, both when it was a French sponsored state, and a Republic, as early as 1954. This would have certainly made life difficult during her time as a member of the ICSC, where she would have been required to be unbiased in her dealings with all sides in the conflict. I am not suggesting for a moment that Canada was ever biased in her work as a member of the ICSC, but merely highlighting the fact that she was potentially in a precarious situation. In fact, five months before she quit the new International Commission of Control and Supervision at the end of July 1973, she extended political recognition of North Vietnam, or the Democratic Republic of Vietnam (7 February 1973).

Another interesting fact highlighting why North Vietnam may have mistrusted Canada and the role she played as part of the ICSC, was that between late 1964 and early 1965, the Canadian Permanent Representative to the ICSC was authorised by the Canadian government to deliver five messages to the North Vietnam on behalf of the United States. These messages indicated that America wanted to bring an end to the war and included the terms under which this could be achieved. The last of these messages was delivered by the Canadians in May 1965, five months before flight F-BELV went missing. The terms offered or suggested by the Americans were, for whatever reason, unacceptable to the authorities of North Vietnam. The other negative aspect of this scenario was how the Canadians would have then been viewed by the North Vietnamese, possibly being seen as not only a neighbour of the United States, but as a trusted ally.

The loss of flight F-BELV and the subsequent search to locate it was always going to be a complicated affair, primarily because of a lack of trust on the part of the North Vietnamese, but also because the role that the ICSC played in Indochina had no real tangible power attached to it. But the first point in need of clarification was, who had primary responsibility to investigate the disappearance of flight F-BELV. It was the lack of any overriding direction in this area which made everything surrounding the search so much more complicated than it should have been.

The rules of the International Civil Aviation Organization (ICAO), a Canadian based organisation, state that the country where the 'accident' occurs has primary responsibility for the subsequent investigation. There were two immediate problems with this 'directive' in the case of flight F-BELV. Firstly, it was officially reported as being missing. As no one knew where the aircraft was there was no way of being able to establish if it had actually crashed, for whatever reason. Secondly, if it had actually crashed or been shot down, it wasn't known in which country that had occurred. This meant that other potential interested parties, such as the manufacturer of the aircraft, in this case Boeing; the country the aircraft was registered in, France; or the nations the aircraft's crew and passengers were from, in this case France, India, Poland and Canada, could not be afforded any particular status in relation to the primary responsibility for carrying out an investigation in to the loss of F-BELV.

The fact that there was a war going on was an added complication in this particular case. Therefore, regardless of ICAO rules and regulations relating to primary responsibility for any investigation, that lay in the hands of whoever Laos and/or, North Vietnam decided it would be. In fact, with three simultaneous overlapping wars in the region, getting an agreement on that was never going to be straightforward. Another point to consider was that a lost aircraft, albeit one from a peacekeeping organisation, wasn't of primary concern to either Laos or North Vietnam. No matter how urgent the matter was for the ICSC, it certainly wasn't a priority for the communist-backed forces operating in both Laos and North Vietnam, and the last thing they wanted or needed was aircraft from other nations flying over their territory and picking up valuable intelligence which they could easily divulge to the American or South Vietnamese authorities.

Although in the immediate aftermath of the loss of F-BELV, and in the subsequent years, both the ICSC and the Canadian authorities made attempts to establish what happened to the aircraft and its personnel, what actions, if any, were taken by the Indian or Polish governments in efforts to establish the whereabouts of flight F-BELV and their countrymen, is unclear.

Ultimately it was the French government who led the investigation, which made sense as the French Ministry of Transportation, National Committee for Aviation Safety (NCAS) was situated in Paris. The aircraft was registered in France and the owners had their headquarters in Paris. The NCAS, having not received any news to the contrary, officially de-registered F-BELV as of 22 September 1971. They also confirmed that they had received no information relating to either the location of a crash site or a reason for its disappearance.

Most of the facts in the case have been covered, along with some of the possible reasons behind the aircraft's disappearance, but there are a few more relevant facts worth considering.

It is confirmed that everything was fine with the aircraft, from the departure at Vientiane until fifteen minutes in to the flight, as that is when Captain Domerque had a radio conversation with the air traffic controllers at Gia Lam Airfield in Hanoi, whilst confirming his flight plan and his estimated time of arrival. At 1521 hours, or just one minute after Captain Domerque had sent his message, Gia Lam sent a reply, but it was not acknowledged by F-BELV. Is this the exact moment that the ICSC aircraft was blown out of the skies? We shall never know for sure, but it is certainly somewhat strange that F-BELV never responded to Gia Lam Airport, which would have been the correct procedure.

At the speed the aircraft was flying at, it would have meant that flight F-BELV had travelled to within approximately 92 nautical miles west of the Laos–North Vietnam border. This would have placed the aircraft somewhere in the region of Ban Thabok, which is situated on the north side of the Mekong River, and still about a 30-minute flight to the Laos–North Vietnam border. Whether it ever made it across the border is not known.

There were hostilities in the air over both Laos and North Vietnam at the time of the disappearance of flight F-BELV, as well as on the ground in Laos. Whether either of these aspects played any part in the loss of F-BELV is an unknown factor.

The official report written by Mr H.G. Pardy of the Department of Foreign Affairs and International Trade, and published on 11 January 1996, with its updated version published in January 2002, gave eight possible reasons as to what caused flight F-BELV to disappear between Vientiane, in Laos and Hanoi in North Vietnam. It is not my intention to repeat in detail what each of these were, although possible reasons are given and comments made on a few of them.

Catastrophic Engine or Other Major Mechanical or Airframe failure. I do not believe that this has any substance to it whatsoever.

Even if all four engines had failed or a wing inexplicably fell off, there would have still been sufficient time for one of the crew to make a radio message.

Explosion within the Aircraft. There is absolutely no credible reason why a member of the crew or any of the passengers would have brought a bomb on board the aircraft, although the author of the report suggests that it is possible. This part of the report also included an interesting, yet debatable aspect that the author of the report had given as a possibility.

> There is no evidence to suggest that any of the parties to the conflict in Indochina felt sufficient animosity toward the ICSC to plan and carry out such an operation. The fact that the ICSC was a marginal player in the eyes of the conflicting parties, makes such a theory a long shot.

The author, I would respectfully suggest has conveniently, or otherwise, missed out a glaring part of the equation. North Vietnam did not necessarily trust the ICSC, certainly not the Canadian delegation who they saw as potential allies of the United States, who they were fighting against and were their sworn enemy. Add to this the possibility that James Sylvester Byrne may or may not have been working as an intelligence officer. If this was the case and North Vietnam knew of his role, then I would suggest that would be a very good reason for them to show sufficient animosity towards the ICSC.

Weather Induced Accident. There is no credible evidence to suggest that inclement weather was responsible for the loss of flight F-BELV.

Navigation Error. I do not see this reason as having any credibility whatsoever, as the crew of F-BELV were very experienced, had flown the route many times before, and the weather was in no way inclement enough to affect the pilot's view of where he was going.

Ground Fire inside Laos. This has always been a possibility, and to suggest otherwise would be slightly naïve.

Air-to-Air Fire over Laos. I do not see this as being a credible suggestion, as if seen by either aircraft of the Royal Laotian Air Force, or the United States Air Force, they would have clearly realised that flight F-BELV was not a military aircraft. The Pathet Lao did possess a number of aircraft, but none were the size of a Stratoliner.

Air-to-Air Fire over North Vietnam. Once again I do not see this as having any credibility as both the North Vietnamese and the United States authorities would have been well aware of the ICSC flights, which were a regular event. Therefore, even allowing for the fact that F-BELV was running a couple of hours late, the authorities in Hanoi knew about this, so why a North Vietnamese aircraft would then shoot it down as it was flying along a designated safe air corridor, defies all common logic. The same explanation can just as equally be applied to the United States.

Ground Fire inside North Vietnam. The North Vietnamese were known to possess some Russian-supplied up-to-date anti-aircraft guns. With this in mind, I believe that it has to be considered as a strong possibility. But allowing for the fact that Hanoi authorities may have forgotten to inform all of its ground forces of the presence of F-BELV, it was a regular flight, flying along an officially designated corridor, so why North Vietnamese ground forces would open fire on a slow-moving, low-flying, non-military aircraft in such an area is unclear and, ultimately, strongly unlikely.

The same report that the above headings were taken from also included a section entitled 'United States Activities on POW/MIA Cases in Indochina', but as F-BELV was more than likely to have been shot out of the sky, the chance of there being any survivors was extremely unlikely.

It is now fifty-four years since flight F-BELV was lost in Indochina, so surely now would be the time for either Laos or Vietnam to come

Flag of Phatet Lao, who were a communist political movement and organisation in Laos.

American Troops enter Cambodia.

Getting the anti-aircraft gun ready in Laos during the US and South Vietnam invasion.

The author's uncle, James Byrne, with his stepson in Italy, 1962.

The cockpit of the 307.

A crashed Boeing 307 Stratoliner, near Alder.

Another angle of the crashed Boeing.

The F-BELV Boeing before it disappeared.

Goods being transported from North to South Vietnam on the Ho Chi Minh trail.

A NVA (North Vietnamese Army) platoon leader.

Boeing 307 Stratoliner.

A wounded
soldier being
aided by
friends.

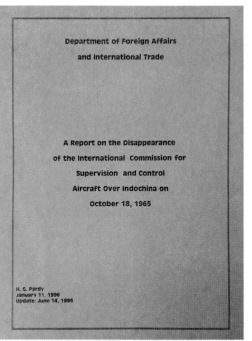

The report on the disappearance
of the international commission
for supervision and control aircraft
over Indochina on October 18,1965.
H. G. Pardy, 1996.

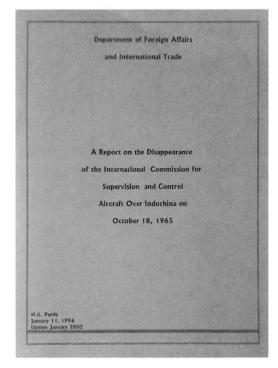

The updated (2002) report from the
Department of Foreign Affairs and
International Trade.

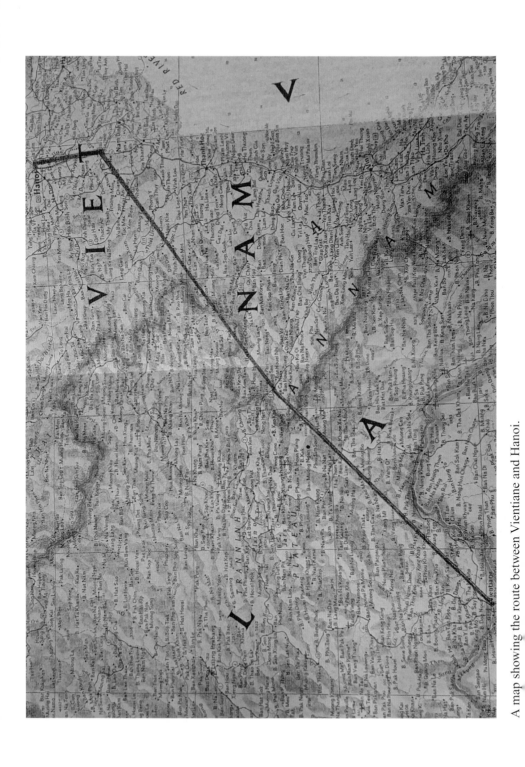

A map showing the route between Vientiane and Hanoi.

clean about what happened to the ICSC aircraft on 18 October 1965, which saw three Canadians lose their lives.

Canada and Vietnam celebrated forty-five years of diplomatic relations in 2018. Bilateral relations between the two countries have been very good due to a large extent to several high-level visits from Canadian officials to Vietnam in recent times, such as Prime Minister Trudeau's November 2017 visit, additionally the announcement of a Canada-Vietnam 'Comprehensive Partnership', which highlighted the two nations' growing relationship in areas such as defence, security and development. As of 2018, there were some 250,000 Vietnamese living in Canada, many having Canadian citizenship. This being the case, it is surprising then that a pointed conversation on the subject has not been had between the two nations.

Chapter 8

Clairvoyant

I gave this chapter quite a lot of thought before deciding whether to include it in the book or not, but will let you, the reader, decide for yourself whether it has any worth or contributes anything to the story of the mystery of flight F-BELV.

I first took an interest in my uncle's death when I was 18 years old in 1976, but it would be another ten years before my inquisitiveness would become more than just that. It was around that time when I first started putting pen to paper on the matter, and began writing to both the Canadian and American authorities; that's what you had to do back then if you wanted to make such an enquiry. Although the first e-mail was sent in 1971, it would still be a few more years before it would become a universally used mode of communication.

Somewhere around the year 2011, I went to see a local lady who lived a fifteen-minute drive away from my home who was a respected clairvoyant or spiritualist. My wife and I went to her house and, after a few introductions and pleasantries, I sat in a small room with the lady. She looked at me and then simply told me things about myself or my life which were connected to a person's name. This did not help me any as, at the time, it would be fair to say that I was somewhat sceptical of such matters, but my wife had consulted her about six months after her father had died, and had found it to be a very positive experience. I had mentioned to my wife that I had always wondered what had happened to my Uncle James, so she encouraged me to have a 'reading' with the lady who, it must be said, certainly wasn't in it for the money as she did the readings free of charge.

My wife and I turned up at the lady's house at the allotted time. I purposely didn't say too much to her to make sure that I didn't give anything away. I told her that my name was David. Despite my scepticism it went well and she told me a few things that wouldn't have been possible for her to know or guess. Here are a couple of examples:

Clairvoyant: 'You are having some cupboards put in.'

Inwardly I was saying to myself, 'How the hell did she know that', with one or two expletives thrown in for good measure. Before responding, I gave myself some time to regain my composure.

'How do you know that?' I asked, careful not to confirm or deny what she had just said.

Clairvoyant: 'Because your mother told me,' she said, without even pausing to take a breath.

At this time my mother had been dead for about eighteen months. I must admit to having had a momentary feeling of indignation as I contemplated what she had just told me.

'My mother?' I repeated. 'Where is she then?'

'She's sat next you,' she replied, indicating to my right hand side. Now, you have to remember she could not have known this information by reading about it, as neither my mother nor I were so important as to be newsworthy.

'OK then, if she's sat next to me, what's her name?'

'Well, it doesn't quite work like that, but hang on a minute.' She looked to where she had indicated my mother was sitting, and nodded her head before turning back to look at me.

'I don't know what you called her, but she's telling me that her name's Angela.'

You could have knocked me down with a feather. My mother's name was Angela, and on that very day we were having our bedroom fitted out with wardrobes and cupboards. It was fair to say that I was suitably impressed. She then mentioned a few other things, which didn't mean anything to me, but then she said

'Does the name James mean anything to you?' I didn't answer, and before I could decide what if anything to say, she continued.

'To start with, I have to tell you, it wasn't his time, he wasn't meant to die.' Her words caught me slightly off guard, like I had been punched around the back of the head by an unknown assailant. I somehow managed to keep my poker face, and did not say a word.

'Did he die in a car crash?' she enquired, making it sound more like a statement than a question.

'I can see debris all over the place,' she paused for a moment, as if she was there soon after it had happened. I didn't say a word, although it was becoming increasingly difficult not to.

'Was it a multi-car pile-up?'

'Why do you ask?'

'Well, there's debris everywhere, and too much of it for just one or two cars, but strangely enough, I can't make out a road.'

I was absolutely gobsmacked. It was blatantly clear to me that she was talking about my Uncle James. It was just a case of when to interrupt her to explain to her what she was actually describing.

'During the Vietnam War in 1965 he was on a flight from Saigon to Hanoi when it was lost, and to this day it has never been recovered.'

'Oh, I see. It all makes sense now, because there was just so much wreckage, it seemed too much for one car having been involved in a crash.'

Soon after that the reading finished and I was about to stand up when the lady said to me, 'Who's Stephen?'

'Pardon?' I said, trying to buy myself a bit of thinking time.

'Your father is telling me to ask you who Stephen is.'

Up until this point there had been no mention of my father at all.

'My father? Where's my father?'

'Over here in the corner,' she said indicating over to my left. This once again brought my indignation to the surface.

'OK, what's his name then?'

She looked over into the corner where she had indicated my father was, nodded her head again, turned to me and said;

'He's asking me to ask you, who is Stephen?'

I could not believe what she was asking me. The hairs on the back of my neck were standing up and my skin went cold.

'He's asked you to ask me who is Stephen?'

She nodded.

The game was up. 'I'm Stephen,' I said feeling somewhat defeated.

'Ah, I get it now,' she said with a smile. She had got so many things right, it was just impossible to ignore, although to this day I still don't know how to explain it. Believe what you will, but without a doubt it was one of the strangest hours of my life.

I did ask her what she had meant when she said, 'It wasn't his time, he wasn't meant to die,' but she was unable to expand

Chapter 9

Air America

Air America was basically an airline which carried both passengers and freight and was owned and operated by the American government between 1950 and 1976, and was a front company of the Central Intelligence Agency throughout the area of Indochina.

Over time it became apparent that the CIA did not have a full-time requirement for the airline, therefore the American government allowed other national agencies and units to also use it. This included the United States Air Force, the United States Army, and the United States Agency for International Development.

In essence Air America was used by the US government to covertly conduct military operations, whilst purporting to be a civilian air carrier, thus allowing it into areas and countries which the United States military could not go to due to treaty restraints contained within the 1954 and 1962 Geneva Accords.

For the three years between 1959 and 1962, Air America provided both direct and indirect support of United States Special Forces operatives, more commonly known as the Green Berets, as part of Project Hotfoot, which provided for the training of members of the Royal Laotian armed forces.

There was a similar operation in place which began in 1962, which saw Army attachés and Air attachés, connected to the United States Embassy in the Laotian capital of Vientiane, which is situated right next to the border with Thailand. This was entitled 'Project 404'. The purpose of which was to keep those American individuals who were on the ground in Laos properly supplied, in order for them to adequately train the Royal Laotian Air Force. Also part of this project were the intriguingly named 'Raven Forward Air Controllers' or 'The Ravens', who were fighter pilots. Their role was to act as forward air control units in covert operations, whilst working alongside operatives of the Central Intelligence Agency in Laos. This included providing information on the exact locations to be targeted during air strikes against ground forces of the communist-led and Hanoi-directed Pathet Lao movement, or elements of the People's Army of Vietnam. Together, Project 404 and The Ravens were collectively known as 'Palace Dog'.

Laos was officially declared a neutral country as a result of the Geneva Accords of 1965 to which both North Vietnam and the United States were signatories. Initially, both countries adhered to the terms of the Geneva Accords. This resulted in the United States removing all of its military personnel from the country, but when North Vietnam did not reciprocate, the prime minister of Laos declared that they had breached the Accords by not removing their troops. At the same time he contacted the United States, requesting that they provide his country with military assistance. As is generally the case with America, they don't and never have done anything small or by half measures. Their assistance came in the shape of Operation Barrel Roll. This was a covert intervention which combined the skill sets of both the United States Air Force 2nd Air Division and the United States Navy Task Force 77, in a close air support campaign in Laos between 14 December 1964 and 29 March 1973.

Initially the intention of the operation was to force North Vietnam to honour the conditions of the 1962 Geneva Accords, which she had signed up to, and to stop her from violating the Laos borders; but she continued to do so. This came in the form of expanding what became known as the Ho Chi Minh Trail, which ran from North Vietnam, through a section of Laos and Cambodia, and into South Vietnam, which allowed the North to keep its troops supplied with weapons, food and other essentials. Latterly the operation turned in to one which provided close air support for the Royal Lao Armed Forces as well as CIA backed tribal mercenaries and elements of the Thai Volunteer Defence Corps, who were a paramilitary unit and part of the Border Patrol Police. They were responsible for border security and preventing counter insurgency.

Amazingly, Operation Barrel Roll was one of the most closely guarded military secrets of what collectively became known as the Vietnam War, and remained so for more than eight years between 14 December 1964 and 29 March 1973. Despite both sides being fully aware of the opposing side's blatant breach of the Geneva Accords of 1962, neither publicized what the other was doing, as each had much to gain by keeping their own role unknown to the outside world which, more importantly on 23 July 1962, in America's case meant the folks back home.

America's involvement in Laos was never intended to be as comprehensive as it turned out to be, the main purpose for their presence being to keep Thailand and Vientiane safe from the threat posed by the North Vietnamese. America's main objective in the region wasn't to engage in combat with the North Vietnamese in Northern Laos, but to keep South Vietnam safe from being overrun by them, but in part they also had to ensure that the North Vietnamese did not totally overrun Laos.

Much of America's plans relied on her belief that the situation with South Vietnam would be resolved, or at least well under control within a year or two, which meant that they only had to prevent the North Vietnamese from taking control of Laos until that time. Once the situation in South Vietnam had become more manageable, then the need to continue supporting Laos would no longer be such a necessity.

The North Vietnamese did not really want to conquer Laos either, all they required was access to a section of the country which their Ho Chi Minh Trail passed through.

For thirteen years, between 1962 and 1975, the aircraft and pilots of Air America were kept very active behind the scenes carrying out operations which were not common knowledge. The regular Royal Laotian military forces were trained by American Special Forces operatives, who were provided with support from Air America. This included inserting and extracting forces at locations where they were needed at any given time. Air America also provided logistical support to Major General Vang Pao of the Royal Lao Army (RLA), and elements of the Thai volunteers whose men were fighting a civil war against the communist-backed Pathet Lao. Part of Air America's purpose was to carry out regular covert reconnaissance missions over North Vietnam in an attempt to locate the whereabouts and activities of the North Vietnamese forces. This was an extremely dangerous operation as if spotted, would have no doubt meant certain death for the CIA operatives on board the aircraft.

There was added danger with any such flight carried out by Air American pilots as, although they came under the control of 7th/13th United States Air Force, none of their aircraft carried military markings of any kind on the fuselage. The Pathet Lao or North Vietnamese would have known which of their own aircraft were in the area, therefore an unmarked aircraft of Air America would have drawn immediate attention.

A further task given to Air America pilots was that of search-and-rescue missions relating to downed US Air Force pilots. Such missions over enemy territory were potentially treacherous as these operations did not have flight plans logged with any of the authorities in the area. All the pilots would have had to go on, if they were lucky, were some co-ordinates. They would then have to try to locate the stricken pilot, land and get them back to safety, before either the Pathet Lao or the North Vietnamese discovered them.

Air America pilots were the only private United States corporate employees who were allowed to fly non-federal, certified military aircraft in a combat role. By the mid-1970s, Air America had acquired two dozen twin-engine transport aircraft along with the same number of short take-off and landing aircraft, as well as thirty helicopters, but these were dedicated to operations in Burma, Cambodia, Thailand and Laos.

This was a massive operation which involved more than 300 people who were employed by Air America as pilots, mechanics, and air freight specialists, who were based all over Indochina, in Laos, Vietnam and Thailand. The combination of so many aircraft and personnel resulted in Air America delivering 21,000 metric tons of much-needed food supplies to Laos, throughout 1970.

Regardless of the perceived rights and wrongs of the CIA-driven Air America working behind the scenes in Indochina, they did a great job. Their area of operations was basically Southeast Asia. During the course of the war they transported animals, food, ammunition, weapons and people, to wherever they were needed.

Animals such as chickens, pigs, water buffalo and cattle needed moving into areas of Vietnam that had been bombarded with the herbicide and defoliant chemical, Agent Orange. For some ten years, between 1961 and 1971, more than 3,100,000 hectares of Vietnam's forest and land had been defoliated. The Red Cross of Vietnam believes that up to one million Vietnamese people suffered severe health problems, including being left disabled by the effects of Agent Orange, although the United States government has challenged these figures. It was and is such a devastating chemical that the children born to those exposed to it, suffered deformities. Even American veterans of the Vietnam War who were exposed to it suffered from leukaemia, Hodgkin's lymphoma and other forms of cancer.

Air America even flew Richard Nixon to different parts of Southeast Asia. They were used to ferry wounded American soldiers to hospital units. They picked up and dropped off spies at the beginning and the end of espionage missions. Diplomats, American commando units, black ops teams and even refugees were ferried about across Indochina. They also carried out food and ammunition drops to troops who had been inserted behind enemy lines. But carrying out such operations came with danger attached to them, not just for the Air America aircraft and crew used to make the drop, but also for those on the ground who the supplies were intended for. Sometimes these units had been operating behind enemy lines on search-and-destroy missions, acting with impunity, because their presence and location had not been known about by the enemy. Helicopters or small aircraft making food and ammunition drops might just as well have set off a flare, as they would be so conspicuous to the enemy

On 30 April 1975 the North Vietnamese finally took over Saigon in South Vietnam. A famous photograph exists which shows a helicopter on the roof of an apartment building 22 Gia Long Street in Saigon. But that wasn't just any old building, it was where all of the United States Agency for International Development employees lived in the city, whilst the top floor was reserved for the CIA's deputy chief of the station. The helicopter also happened to belong to Air America, who were right there until the very end, still trying to do the very best that they could.

The civil war which took place in Laos between 1959 and 1975, is known as the Secret War by the CIA operatives from the Special Activities Division and Hmong veterans who were involved in it. This armed struggle was eventually won by the Pathet Lao, communist-backed rebels and North Vietnamese fighters, who eventually defeated the forces of the Royal Lao Government. Fearing severe retribution from Pathet Lao forces, it is estimated that some 300,000 Laotian civilians fled to neighbouring Thailand to claim sanctuary. This left the CIA-backed Hmong rebels, who had fought alongside government forces before Laos had fallen to the Pathet Lao, to continue the fight.

The Hmong people are an ethnic group of East and Southeast Asia, who had depended on the cultivation of their poppy crops to use as a form of currency, and it had been the CIA who had worked to help prepare the Hmong to fight against the Pathet Lao.

The main area in Laos where the Hmong had grown and cultivated their poppy fields had been an area known as the Plain of Jars, the name coming from its rocky megalithic landscape. When this was captured by the Pathet Lao in 1964, the Royal Laotian Air Force, whom the Hmong had depended on to collect their opium, did not have small enough aircraft to enable them to land quickly on one of the dirt runways, collect the Hmong's drugs, and make good their escape. Without their opium they had no way of being able to sustain themselves. The next part of the story is a bit more difficult to tell, so I will use the phrase 'it is alleged' that Air America aircraft *were* used to transport the Hmong's opium from the Plain of Jars area of Laos to General Vang Pao's headquarters at Long Tieng. There are two questions which remain unclarified. Firstly, were Air America and the CIA directly involved in physically collecting and transporting the drugs, or did they allow others to use their aircraft to move the drugs? The second question is, did either Air America or the CIA directly profit from the movement of these drugs?

The relevance of mentioning the Hmong people, is that the CIA were involved in training them to fight against the Pathet Lao and North Vietnamese forces, and there was even a story that one CIA operative had taken a Hmong woman as his wife and had four children with her. The operative concerned remained behind when the United States left Vietnam, and lived with his wife and children in Thailand, before eventually returning to America in the 1990s.

In 1990 a film entitled *Air America* was released, starring Mel Gibson and Robert Downey Jr., directed by Roger Spottiswoode, and based on the best-selling, non-fictional book, *Air America* (1979), written by British writer and journalist Christopher Robbins. In the film, Gibson and Downey Jr. are Air America pilots flying missions in

Laos during the Vietnam War, when they discover that their aircraft is being used to smuggle heroin by 'government agents'.

There were concerns in certain circles that there were those in the Laotian military who had used the war and the CIA to make themselves rich from the opium trade.

There is no doubt that throughout the conflict in Indochina, during the period of the Vietnam War, Air America proved to be an invaluable asset for the United States.

Chapter 10

Central Intelligence Agency

The Central Intelligence Agency, better known as the CIA, was officially established on 18 September 1947 and is a foreign intelligence service of the United States government. Its operatives, or members, are civilian and the agency has no law enforcement capacity. Its purpose is to gather, process and analyse intelligence and information on a global scale which may impact on, or have a direct effect on, the national security of the United States of America. It reports to the Director of National Intelligence, who is a member of the Cabinet and sits on the National Security Council, who in turn report directly to the President of the United States.

In its original format it began life as the Office of Strategic Services, and came under the command of Lieutenant-Colonel Archimedes Leonidas Attilio Patti, who headed American operations in Kunming, China, and Hanoi, Vietnam in 1945. It is interesting to note that back then Patti worked closely with the Viet Minh who during the Vietnam War opposed both South Vietnam and the United States. The Viet Minh's leader and founding father was Ho Chi Minh, who later became the president of North Vietnam.

In an interview he gave in 1981, Archimedes Patti said the following about the Vietnam War:

> In my opinion the Vietnam War was a great waste.
> There was no need for it to happen in the first place.
> At all. None whatsoever. During all the years of

the Vietnam War no one ever approached me to find out what happened in 1945 or 44. In all the years I spent in the Pentagon, Department of State in the White House, never was I approached by anyone in authority. However, I did prepare a large number, and I mean about, oh, well over fifteen position papers on our position in Vietnam. But I never knew what happened to them. Those things just disappeared, they just went down the dry well.

As has been mentioned elsewhere in this book Air America and the CIA were intrinsically linked. It would be fair to say that the CIA would have struggled to have been an effective entity throughout Indochina without the aircraft of Air America.

In 1965 the CIA set up and put in to action the Phoenix Program, which also involved elements of the United States Special Operations Forces (SOF), the United States Army intelligence collection units, Australian Special Forces, and South Vietnam's security forces. The purpose of the program was to identify and destroy members of the Viet Cong, also known as the People's Liberation Armed Forces of South Vietnam, who operated throughout South Vietnam and Cambodia, and during the Vietnam War fought against the United States and South Vietnam's government forces.

The program achieved its aims through a combination of ways, some of which would have appeared distasteful or excessive to armchair warriors back home in the United States. The methods used to identify and destroy Viet Cong members included infiltration of their ranks, capture, interrogation and assassination. To achieve its aims the program had two wings, the Provincial Reconnaissance Units (PRUs) and the regional interrogation centres. The members of the PRUs would go out on targeted patrols, actively looking for those believed to be active members of the Viet Cong. Depending on the circumstances, when they came across such individuals they would either be killed or captured. This also included civilians who it was believed were either Viet Cong sympathisers or who might have information on their activities or whereabouts. Those who were taken to the interrogation centres were rumoured to have been tortured in an effort to illicit relevant information from them about the Viet Cong in their area. Any information obtained from these prisoners was fed back to the PRUs for them to be tasked with acting on it, which usually meant going out and capturing or killing more of those suspected of being Viet Cong. Those who were captured, in reality, only had two main choices, defect or be killed.

The Phoenix Program ran from 1965 to 1972, during which time 81,740 suspected Viet Cong operatives, informants, and their supporters were either captured and 'persuaded' to defect, or killed. During the same time period the Viet Cong killed some 33,000 South Vietnamese, village officials and civil servants.

What has to be remembered here is that the Phoenix Program was in the main targeted at a civilian population, and not at enemy soldiers, although in what was after all a guerrilla-type war, the line that constituted an enemy soldier could easily become blurred.

Under the Phoenix Program a person could be arrested and prosecuted if suspected of being a communist, or of supporting communism in some way. This was allowed under special laws, but to ensure that it wasn't abused with phoney accusations for personal or business reasons, there had to be three sources of evidence to convict someone who had been identified as a communist. Those found guilty could be imprisoned for two years.

This was a difficult balancing act for the CIA, and others involved in the program, to get right. On the one hand the American authorities were pushing their hearts and minds strategy, in an effort to win the support of the civilian population. In an attempt to avoid alienating themselves in the eyes of the Vietnamese people, they had to tread carefully with such as the Phoenix Program. The heavy-handed large-scale approach where groups of individuals were rounded up, arrested, and detained for long periods of time, most being innocent of any offence, didn't help the American cause at all. Tactics had to change, there was no option. Political killings, where carried out, had to be targeted to just one individual, and quickly justified.

The methods of torture used at the interrogation centres allegedly included such acts as rape, gang rape, and sometimes rape followed by murder, if the suspect didn't talk. There were cases of electric shock treatment with electrodes being attached to the genitals, nipples or tongue. Suspects had their arms tied behind their backs and were then hung up with their feet off the ground. There was water torture, beating, and dogs were used for mauling.

In Jennifer Harbury's 2005 book *Truth, Torture, and the American way: The History and Consequences of U.S. Involvement in Torture*, it mentions that the acts of reported torture were carried out by South Vietnamese forces, with CIA operatives and special forces personnel being present, but only playing a supervisory role. Whether that means they were simply observing the events, or advising the South Vietnamese interrogators what to do, is not clear.

Vincent Hichiro Okamoto acquired a law degree from the University of Southern California in 1971, before going on to become a prosecutor and privately practising law. On 15 April 2002 he was appointed to the Los Angeles Superior Court bench by Governor Joseph Graham Davis of California.

During the Vietnam War, Okamoto received a commission as a 2nd Lieutenant in the United States Army, having passed through the Reserve Officers' Training Corps (ROTC). He then received Ranger training, before being sent out to Vietnam. While attached to Company B of the 2nd Battalion, 27th Infantry Regiment, 25th Infantry Division, he was assigned to the Phoenix Program for two months as an intelligence liaison officer. With regard to his work in that role, he said:

The problem was, how do you find the people on the blacklist? It's not like you had the address and telephone number. The normal procedure would be to go into a village and just grab someone and say, 'Where's Nguyen so and so?' Half the time the people were so afraid they would not say anything. Then a Phoenix team would take the informant, put a sandbag over his head, poke out two holes so he could see, put commo wire around his neck like a long leash, and walk him through the village and say, 'When we go by Nguyen's house scratch your head.' Then that night Phoenix would come back, knock on the door, and say, 'April Fool, motherfucker.' Whoever answered the door would get wasted. As far as they were concerned whoever answered was a Communist, including family members. Sometimes they'd come back with ears to prove that they killed people.

Vincent Okamoto was a recipient of the Distinguished Service Cross, America's second highest military award that can be given to a member of the United States Army, for acts of extreme gallantry and the risking of one's life in combat with the enemy.

It will come as no surprise when I say that the Phoenix Program was virtually unheard of during the time it was actually in existence, and not only were the American public not aware of what was being done in their name, neither were the majority of American officials in Washington. It was brought into the main stream only in 1970 when Ed Murphy, who had been a military intelligence officer in the United States Army, publicly criticized the Phoenix Program. This led to a series of US Congressional hearings the following year, where stories of murder on an almost industrial scale, as well as accounts of torture, were recounted time and again by ex-CIA operatives or military personnel. The military command in Vietnam announced that the Program was in keeping with South Vietnamese law, and complied with the laws of land warfare.

A former CIA analyst, Samuel A. Adams, gave an interview to CBC News, during which he spoke candidly about how the Phoenix Program was, in essence, a licence to kill people as they saw fit. These practices also included cases of torture.

As a result of the Congressional hearings the CIA Phoenix Program was officially closed down, only for the South Vietnamese government to continue with it under the title of Plan F-6.

All this goes a long way to showing just how cheap and meaningless life had become, when people who had the power could so easily kill those who didn't. It is sad to think that no one stood up and said, 'Enough, no more killing.' It is sobering to think that certain CIA operatives could carry out their work as coldly as they did, before attempting to justify their actions by stating that they were lawful because they were in line with Vietnamese law.

With all these events, it is no surprise that flight F-BELV was lost, quite likely brought down by unexpected ground fire, whether that was in Pathet Lao-occupied territory inside Laos, or over North Vietnam. This had been a regular weekly flight for many months, so it would have been a recognisable aircraft, flying at its usual low altitude along the same agreed flight path; so why shoot it down? However it met its fate, it must have been instantaneous, and disabled the cockpit, as why was no radio message sent, to the effect that it was under attack, along with its location at the time?

Whatever the circumstances behind the downing of flight F-BELV, the likelihood of it being a case of mistaken identity can only be guessed at. Although the shooting down of the aircraft was almost certainly intentional, there can be little doubt that whoever shot it down did so in the belief that they were shooting at an aircraft other than one which belonged to the ICSC.

In August 1965 the South Vietnamese Prime Minister, Phan Huy Quat, resigned. This caused huge concern to the CIA as they feared that this would rekindle religious issues between the minority Catholics and the Buddhists, which had been apparent under the country's previous Prime Minister, Ngo Dinh Diem. On 1 November 1963, Ngo Dinh Diem had been assassinated along with his brother, Ngo Dinh Nhu, by Nguyen Van Nhung, who at the time was the bodyguard of the leader of the Army of the Republic of Vietnam, General Duong Van Minh, who, following what many have claimed was a CIA-backed coup d'état, became the President of South Vietnam.

The CIA became concerned that there could be future problems within the country due to Buddhists being, almost openly, overlooked in preference to Catholics, especially when it came to government and military positions. What was of most concern to the CIA was that these religious differences might be exploited by the Communists, who would use the divide in the community to expand their influence amongst the people.

The irony here was that the biggest influence in South Vietnamese politics, wasn't communism, but the continuous interference by elements of the CIA.

Chapter 11

Searches

Many searches have been carried out in relation to flight F-BELV, not only in the immediate aftermath of its disappearance, but also over the subsequent years. Despite all these efforts, no trace of the aircraft has ever been found, nor the bodies of any of those who were on board.

On the evening of **19 October 1965**, the North Vietnamese authorities reported that the information on the flight had been communicated to the relevant officials, organisations and people who were situated along the corridor of the aircraft's flight path. They, in turn, were ordered to search for the missing aircraft. Early on the morning of 20 October 1965, the ICSC Bureau in Hanoi again officially requested permission for two Commission aircraft to be allowed to carry out search activities over North Vietnamese territory. The request was for flights on both **20 and 21 October 1965**.

During the afternoon of 20 October, North Vietnamese officials informed the ICSC's representatives in Hanoi that the government was taking all possible measures and using all necessary means to carry out the search, both on the ground and in the air. That evening, North Vietnamese officials informed the ICSC that a search had been conducted along the length of the corridor between Hanoi and Muong Xen, in Nam Ha Province, and that no aircraft wreckage had been discovered. It was a very interesting reply by the North Vietnamese authorities, because in it they didn't actually answer the request by the ICSC, for two of its aircraft to be allowed to carry out search activities along the corridor of F-BELV's flight path over North Vietnamese territory. Rather than stating 'yes' or 'no' to the request, they just provided the answer that they wanted to give. The reality of the situation was, they were never going to allow an organisation such as the ICSC, who they strongly believed were in cahoots with the Americans, to fly over their territory to conduct a search, during which time photographs would have undoubtedly been taken from the aircraft of the ground below.

On 21 October, North Vietnamese authorities once again contacted the ICSC and advised them that further searches had been conducted in Thanh Hoa and Ninh Binh provinces, and that nothing had been discovered. Not to be deterred, officials from the ICSC once again requested permission for personnel from the Commission to be allowed to accompany the North Vietnamese search parties, both on the ground and in the air. No reply was ever received in relation to that request.

In October 1965, anti-war demonstrations began in the United States. It would be another eight years before the last American troops put down their weapons, bringing an end to their nation's military presence in Indochina.

In **November 1965**, less than one month after F-BELV's disappearance, the wife of Mr John Douglas Turner, one of the Canadians on board the aircraft at the time of its disappearance, travelled to North Vietnam to speak with officials in an effort to glean any further information about her husband and the others who were on board. The North Vietnamese were supportive, said all the right things, but were unable to offer any further information other than what was already known about the situation.

On **7 February 1973** ten members of the Canadian Red Cross arrived in Vietnam to assist in the release of captured military and foreign civilian personnel in North Vietnam. On the same day, the Secretary of State for External Affairs in the Canadian government announced that he hoped the establishment of diplomatic relations with North Vietnam would greatly help with the investigation in to the loss of flight F-BELV and all those on board the aircraft at the time.

Just six weeks later on **18 March 1973**, the Secretary of State for External Affairs visited North Vietnam and raised the matter of the missing F-BELV with their authorities. They had no further information other than what was already known about the missing aircraft. The Vietnamese foreign minister said that further enquiries would be undertaken.

It would have been highly unlikely that the Vietnamese authorities were about to find out any new information on the matter, eight years after it had taken place; they either knew what happened to F-BELV or they didn't. If they didn't know in 1965, it was doubtful that they would know in 1973. There was, of course, the possibility that they knew a great deal about the fate of F-BELV, but didn't want to say because that would mean they were either responsible for bringing down F-BELV or complicit in covering up its disappearance. There was also the possibility that the Canadian government had got it wrong in their assumption that North Vietnam could help them with their enquiries relating to F-BELV, because maybe, just maybe, it hadn't come down in North Vietnam at all, but in neighbouring Laos.

In March 1973, relations between Canada and North Vietnam were not in a particularly good state of affairs, and this culminated in the North Vietnamese refusing to accept the Canadian Ambassador in Hanoi.

On **27 November 1974** a meeting took place in Beijing, China, between the Canadian Ambassador, Mr Charles John Small, and the ambassador for North Vietnam, where the issue of flight F-BELV was raised. Ambassador Small enquired about the inquiry that had been promised to the Canadian Secretary of State for Foreign Affairs on 18 March 1973. Despite the twenty months which had elapsed since then, the North Vietnamese Ambassador said that he had no new information to pass on, although he expressed his sympathy for the relatives of the missing Canadians. During the conversation the North Vietnamese ambassador pointed out that F-BELV would have had to pass over Laos as well as North Vietnam en route to Hanoi, the inference being that the aircraft could have just as easily been lost over Laos as North Vietnam. He also drew attention to the fact that the terrain in both countries was of a 'difficult nature'. He promised to request Hanoi to provide any additional information that might be available or come to light.

On **6 January 1975**, the North Vietnamese Embassy in Beijing sent a diplomatic note to the Canadian Embassy, which referred to the meeting and discussion of 27 November 1974:

> Upon learning the missing of the I.C plane on October 18, 1965, the responsible authorities of the Government of the Democratic Republic of Viet Nam, have tried to find the trace of the plane. On October 20 and 22, 1965, the Liaison Mission of the High Command of the Viet Nam People's Army to the International Commission for Supervision and Control in its notes No.519 and 522, informed the Commission that the Government of the Democratic Republic of Viet Nam had conducted several intensive searches but no trace of the plane was found.
>
> The Government of the Democratic Republic of Viet Nam has continued to pay attention to this accident, but has got no further information about the missing plane.

There was no mention of the promised inquiry made at the meeting on 18 March 1973. On receipt of the above note, the Canadian diplomat who had received it took the opportunity to enquire about any new information in the F-BELV case. He was informed by the Vietnamese diplomat that the 'investigation had been completed'.

A week after the Note was delivered, the Canadian Ambassador in Beijing, Mr Charles John Small, had a conversation with another Vietnamese diplomat, and was told that the aircraft 'could not have crashed in North Vietnam,' although there was no detailed explanation attached to those comments.

Later the same month, the Canadian ambassador to Laos also raised the matter with the Laotian foreign minister as well as the resident ambassador of North Vietnam. The Laotian foreign minister promised that he would 'reply in due course'. No such reply was ever received from the Laotian government.

On **20 September 1977**, a diplomatic note was sent to the Socialist Republic of Vietnam in Saigon, by the Canadian ambassador. Similar notes were also sent to the governments of India, Poland and France, to see what information they may have obtained in relation to F-BELV. Not one of these countries replied to the Canadian correspondence.

The sad fact surrounding this is that someone, somewhere, knows the fate of flight F-BELV but, for political reasons, has never come forward with an explanation as to what happened. This is possibly to save political face, and to make an admission now all these years later would prove to be politically embarrassing, as well as damaging to a country's name.

A report was drawn up by Mr H.G. Pardy of the Department of Foreign Affairs and International Trade, which was dated 11 January 1996, entitled, 'A Report on the Disappearance of the International Commission for Supervision and Control Aircraft over Indochina on October 18, 1965.' This report was in turn updated in January 2002. Below is an abridged version of that report, although the essence of what it says is the same as the original report.

Update of Activities on the search for F-BELV
(December 2001)

'Since 1998, some thirty-five years after the loss of flight F-BELV, efforts have continued to locate its crash site.' As recorded elsewhere in this book, the aircraft disappeared on a flight between Vientiane, the capital of Laos, and Hanoi, the capital of Vietnam, on 18 October 1965. 'The aircraft was carrying four crew and nine members of the International Commission for Supervision and Control, including three Canadians.'

'The Director General of Consular Affairs for Canada contacted the United States Department of Defence Prisoner of War/Missing in Action Group in January 1996. The reason for this was to ask if they were in possession of any information on the disappearance of F-BELV. The Joint Task Force Full-Accounting (JTF-FA) Office, subsequently conducted a search of its own records and provided information on the possible location of the crash site.'

It is interesting to note here that America had not been forthcoming with this information and only provided it when asked, by the Canadian government, to check their records. Although, without suggesting for one moment that the Americans had done this intentionally, it still seems somewhat strange that they had not come forward with this information sooner, especially in a case which they must have known was still an active one for the Canadians.

The information was:

A B-377 crashed in the vicinity of 19'11"N 104'10"E on October 19, 1965. The B-377 is similar to F-BELV in that they are both four engine, propeller driven cargo/

passenger aircraft. No other similar aircraft were lost in Laos or Vietnam on or about October 18, 1965. The location is approximately 24 kilometres off the planned flight route and just west of the Laotian-Vietnamese border.

JFT-FA also discovered a possible correlation between four refugee reports relating to the crash of a large aircraft in the early to mid-sixties near the location noted above.

After receiving this information, the Canadian Embassy in Thailand was instructed to approach the government of Laos, as well as the resident United States Missing in Action team in Laos, with a view to being allowed to visit the site that had been identified by the United States in 1998. It was requested by the Canadian government that some of their own people be allowed to take part in any subsequent search team. Initially, the government of Laos agreed to this and gave their permission for a joint United States-Canada search team, but this permission was withdrawn due to an unspecified security concern in the search area.

In early December 1998, the government of Laos advised the Canadians that it was prepared to visit the crash site using its own facilities and resources, to conduct a search. However, there was a slight catch. The Laotians requested that the Canadian government reimburse them for the incremental expenses involved, this included the use of a helicopter. The Canadian government, although possibly somewhat surprised at the Laotian request, agreed to it.

The Laotians sent a team to the identified area and carried out a search which took place between 15 and 30 December 1998. The search included Laotian officials interviewing local residents and their families, who had lived in the area going back to October 1965, or who had visited the crash site. The Laotian search team had travelled to the general area of the crash, before then undertaking a 6-mile hike to the exact identified location of Xaylayleng Mountain situated in the country's Moark district.

It is interesting to note that even thirty-five years after the event, the Laotian government were still not willing to allow Canadian authorities to either conduct their own search or be part of one led by a Laotian search team. Still something to hide possibly, after so many years.

During the search by the Laotian authorities, wreckage from an aircraft was discovered, which included a part number and a manufacturer's identification mark. Besides this, five small bone fragments were also recovered. Still photographs of the crash site were taken by the search team, along with a video of the mission. These were forwarded on to Canadian authorities. The video, not so much to assist in the identification of the aircraft, but to convey how difficult and challenging the terrain was in which the search team had been operating.

The photographs that were taken of the wreckage were of several different pieces which were believed to be from an aircraft of the period 1938–1939, when Boeing 307 aircraft were constructed.

The one piece of wreckage that the Laotian authorities sent to Ottawa, along with photographs and a video, were forwarded on to the Transportation Safety Board of Canada, where they were examined by Mr K.M. Picwick, Chief of Materials and Structures. Afterwards he submitted an engineering report regarding his examination which was signed and dated 20 September 1999. His report included the following.

> An enquiry was addressed to Alcoa, Mill Products Division, requesting identification of their product and a possible date or period of manufacture. Alcoa have concluded that the absolute earliest date of use of the material cannot be established, but on the basis of the

dates at which the various products designators and standard identifiers were introduced, they believe that the likely time period for mill production for the alloy sheet material was the early 1940's to the early 1960s. This finding would seem to preclude the wreckage being part of the original B307 manufacture, but does not exclude those parts added post Second World War.

This report led the Department of Foreign Affairs and International Trade to approach the Boeing Aircraft Company in Seattle for its assistance in identifying the piece of wreckage which had been sent by the Laotian authorities. At the time, Boeing was refurbishing the last B-307 aircraft for display at the National Air and Space Museum in Washington DC. Mr Mark Kempton, supervisor of the Stratoliner Restoration Project, agreed to carry out the examination of the piece of wreckage. To assist him further, the photographs and video which had also been sent by the Laotian authorities, were also forwarded on to him.

After conducting his examination on the piece of wreckage, he forwarded a report to the Canadian Consulate General in Seattle. The report was signed and dated 7 September 2000, and included the following comments.

As the manager in charge of the recovery and restoration for Stratoliner, it has availed me to a large amount of information about the ten Stratoliners built by Boeing. Including details like engineering documents and specifications, drawings, operations manuals, maintenance manuals, pictures and of course NC 19903. With this information available to us, we do not believe the wreckage indicated above belongs to F-BELV or any other Boeing S-307 Stratoliner. Again this is based on the video, pictures and the piece of Wreckage.

After twice having the piece of wreckage examined by two independent experts, the Department of Foreign Affairs sought the assistance of the government of Vietnam for any information it may have on the matter which was first discussed with the Vietnamese authorities on a visit by the Director General of Consular Affairs to Hanoi in October 2000. The matter was further discussed during a visit in March 2001, and again at discussions in Ottawa in June 2001. As of January 2002, the Vietnamese authorities had still not conducted, or allowed the Canadian authorities to conduct, a search for flight F-BELV.

The JTF-FA Office of the Department of Defence, in the United States, was once again contacted, it is believed sometime in late 2001, at which time they agreed to further research the matter and provide any additional information it may discover.

Chapter 12

1965 and all that

As flight F-BELV went missing in 1965, it may be useful to take a look at that year in more detail. This will give a flavour of the state of the war as it developed, from the first landing of American combat troops in Vietnam, to the disappearance of the ICSC aircraft on 18 October 1965.

By 1965, the Viet Cong were not only well established, they were well trained and organised, and numbered somewhere between 50,000 and 80,000; these were mainly men, but there were also a number of women. By **March 1965**, and working alongside the Viet Cong, were the North Vietnamese Army (NVA), who numbered 5,800 men. These were split into three regiments.

Although American advisors had been in Vietnam for many years, going back to the early 1950s, action began in earnest on **2 March 1965**, when America decided that the talking, threats and counter threats had finally run their course. They sent 100 bomber aircraft from Da Nang, to attack identified military targets in North Vietnam. This was the beginning of what was codenamed Operation Rolling Thunder.

Just one week later, on **9 March 1965**, and just one day after 3,500 US Marines had landed at Da Nang, United States aircraft began using napalm on bombing raids over North Vietnam, after being given the go ahead by American President, Lyndon B. Johnson.

On **23 March 1965**, Great Britain pledged her support for President Johnson's policy in Vietnam. There were two reasons for this, and sadly one of the reasons was monetary. With America being one of Britain's biggest allies, Britain really had no option but to offer her support. The second reason was that Britain was also concerned about the spread of communism throughout Southeast Asia, and felt that if South Vietnam fell to the Viet Cong and North Vietnamese, then her interests and investments in the region would be lost in their entirety.

There have been unsubstantiated claims that British Special Forces did in fact serve in Vietnam, not necessarily as British soldiers, but in a covert capacity and serving as American soldiers. That would be an extremely interesting story in its own right.

The four United States naval vessels of Amphibious Task Force 76 had left Japan during the last week of **January 1965**, and after six weeks at sea they finally arrived off the east coast of Vietnam. It was just after 9 am on **8 March 1965**. In total there were 3,500 United States Marines from the 9th Marine Expeditionary Brigade (MEB), waiting patiently on board the vessels, USS *Mount McKinley*, USS *Henrico*, USS *Union* and USS *Vancouver*, just offshore in the turbulent waters of the South China Sea. The task force's commanding officer, General Frederick J. Karch, was a veteran of the Second World War and the battles against the Japanese at Saipan, Tinian and Iwo Jima. But this was going to be an amphibious landing the likes of which he had certainly never experienced. At the allotted hour the United States Marines stormed ashore, uncertain of what they would be confronted with. Intelligence reports had warned of Viet Cong having large numbers of fighters all over Da Nang. General Karch feared the worst, he knew that if the Viet Cong had set up their defences properly then more of his men would become casualties, a scenario which he feared the most. He knew that by the time his tour of Vietnam was over, there would be a number of letters he would have to write to grieving parents back home, but he didn't want to be writing hundreds of them just one day after his arrival.

It was a cool morning as the men began making their way from the boats across the beach, their only adversary being a steady drizzle, as they waited for the first wave of Viet Cong bullets to tear through their ranks. But as it turned out they were not met by any armed resistance. There were no darkly-clad oriental men, in bamboo and palm-leaf conical-shaped hats, wearing flip flops and bearing Kalashnikovs. The only people waiting for them were the Mayor of Da Nang, a number of camera crews, a few excited newspaper reporters, and some pretty young Vietnamese women holding garlands of flowers. The marines, who were mentally ready for the fury of battle, were left confused and unsure of what was happening, but it soon became clear that their intelligence reports had been way off the mark. In just over an hour the amphibious landing craft had delivered 1,400 heavily-laden, ready for anything, American Marines on to the beaches at Da Nang.

With that morning's new arrivals, there were now some 26,500 American 'military advisors' in Vietnam, these were Marines, Air Force personnel and those from Special Forces. But these advisors were not there to fight a war, at least that's what the rule book said. Yes, they could shoot back if fired upon, but they were not to become involved in firefights with the Viet Cong. They were there to support South Vietnam's own troops as the United States Special Forces, in the form of the Green Berets, had been doing since 1957, as it was after all their war and not America's. By 1965 Special Forces had more than fifty detachments in South Vietnam, many of which were situated along the border with Cambodia. Their main purpose was to provide military-style training to local tribesmen and to prevent infiltration by Viet Cong guerrillas from across the border in Cambodia and Laos.

The soldiers and military leaders of the South Vietnamese army could not be described as being gung ho, they were much happier remaining in the comparative safety of their garrison outposts. These were simple constructions with mud walls and a perimeter fence made of nothing sturdier than bamboo stakes. The Viet Cong used fear as their most potent weapon. Where were they? Most of the time, right under the noses of the American and South Vietnamese soldiers, but for them there were no khaki-green uniforms with military flashes to identify a particular regiment or rank. They were elusive, and trying to find them was once described as 'looking for tears in a bucket of water'.

So far, Vietnam had been seen as not too bad a posting. Up until February 1965, the American advisors could even have their families come and visit them for a week or so. Although the fighting continued, it wasn't yet on a scale that it would ultimately reach. The same week in which the American Marines arrived, there had been a battle at an isolated South Vietnamese army camp near the village of Binh Dinh, where the Viet Cong had hurled themselves at the camp's perimeter fence in an almost suicidal attack, which had continued for almost six hours. By the time it was over, an estimated 500 of them had been killed.

The arrival of the 3,500 American Marines had not been a coincidence nor just an increase in American advisors for the sake of it. They had been sent because of an incident which had taken place on **7 February 1965**, which had left 7 American servicemen dead and more than 100 of them wounded.

Camp Holloway was situated near Pleiku, where there was also a massive United States air base. Holloway was the temporary home to 400 American servicemen of the 52nd Combat Aviation Battalion where, on the hot and humid night of **7 February 1965**, they were asleep in their beds. The previous week there had been an official ceasefire due to a religious festival, which had provided the Americans with some welcome down time. As for the Viet Cong, they had used the time to prepare for a surprise attack on the unsuspecting Americans at Camp Holloway. At 2 am, all hell broke loose, at least that's what it would have felt like to the young

Americans, as the Viet Cong began their attack with mortars and machine-gun fire. In the ensuing confusion the camp was left devastated as ammunition dumps exploded, aircraft were set alight and buildings were destroyed, before the Viet Cong disappeared, as quickly as they had appeared.

An incensed American President, Lyndon B. Johnson, said, 'They are killing our men while they sleep in the night.' He stated, 'I can't ask our American soldiers to continue to fight with one hand behind their back.'

Without doubt, 1965 was the defining year for America's involvement in Vietnam. At the start of the year there were 23,000 military advisors, and by the end of December there were 184,300 military personnel.

On **30 March 1965**, a car bomb explodes in front of the American Embassy in Saigon. The bomb kills 22 people including two Americans and a further 183 people are injured.

Between **3** and **5 April 1965**, Operation Rolling Thunder is extended to cover the attack of non-military targets in North Vietnam, it is not known what the justification for this is.

On **4 April 1965**, 258 Viet Cong are killed in the U Minh Forest, in an attack spear-headed by the South Vietnamese army, United States forces acting 'purely' in a support capacity.

On **7 April 1965**, less than a month after 3,500 United States Marines had landed at Da Nang, President Lyndon B. Johnson says America is ready to begin 'unconditional discussions' to end the war. The announcement also includes the offer of a $1 billion aid programme that would cover the entirety of Southeast Asia.

On **11 April 1965**, just four days after President Johnson had made his offer, the North Vietnamese authorities reply in the negative, and turn the offer down. This would result in ten more years of fighting and the deaths of tens of thousands of both military and civilian personnel.

On **15 April 1965**, the biggest air raid of the entire war takes place and involves some 230 South Vietnamese and American fighter-bomber aircraft that drop 1000lb of bombs on a Viet Cong stronghold.

On **21 April 1965**, a Buddhist monk commits suicide by setting himself on fire in a Saigon street, as a way of demonstrating against the war. Pictures of the monk on fire are seen all around the world.

On **28 April 1965**, the United States Secretary of Defence, Robert McNamara, announces that the war was costing America $1.5 billion a year.

Between **3 and 5 May 1965**, the first United States Army combat unit, in the shape of 3,500 men of the 173rd Airborne Brigade, arrived in Vietnam.

On **5 May 1965**, the United States Army, 173rd Airborne Brigade, were sent to Bien Hoa, which is on the outskirts of Saigon. In late July they were joined by the men of the 1st Brigade, 101st Airborne Division. On 26 May, American soldiers were joined by their Australian cousins, when 800 of them arrived in Vietnam to join the fight.

On **10 May 1965**, South Vietnamese troops retreat during a battle with the Viet Cong, after having been spooked by the sound of their own aircraft flying overhead.

Viet Cong forces had, for a short period of time, occupied the provincial capital of Song Be situated about 60 miles north of Saigon, on **11 May 1965**.

America halts the bombing of North Vietnam on **13 May 1965**, to see if Hanoi will compromise on peace conditions. With guerrilla attacks increasing on a daily basis, and on the same day that the Viet Cong stage a daylight raid on a textile mill on the outskirts of Saigon, this once again met with a negative response, and so America resumed her bombing of North Vietnam on **19 May 1965**.

On **29 May 1965**, the South Vietnamese 51st Regiment is virtually wiped out in a surprise attack by the Viet Cong.

On **18 June 1965**, the Americans deploy B-52 Stratofortress bomber aircraft of the 133rd Provisional Wing of the United States Air Force for the first time in Southeast Asia, as part of Operation Arc Light. They took off from Andersen Air Force Base on the island of Guam to strike North Vietnamese and Viet Cong strongholds, some 3,000 miles away in North Vietnam.

Flying over the South China Sea just before dawn, the twenty-seven aircraft approached the coastline of Da Nang. Cruising at some 40,000 feet, they went unseen and unheard by anyone on the ground. As they reached the co-ordinates of the location they had been given to attack, the captain of each B-52 bomber flicked his bomb-arming switch on the panel in front of him, to 'on'. This one simple action had immediately armed all eighty-four of the 500lb bombs carried in the belly of the aircraft, along with the twenty-four 750lb bombs carried underneath the wings. In a matter of seconds the payload from each aircraft had been released. Those unfortunate enough to be below would have had no idea that they were about to be blown to oblivion. Having accomplished the mission, the B-52s, or the 'BUFFs' (Big Ugly Fat Fellows) as their crews liked to call them, made their turns and headed for home which, on this occasion, was the island of Guam.

Three of the B-52 bombers were lost on that first raid. Two of them collided with each other, whilst the third was lost due to being unable to carry out a mid-air refuel.

On **15 July 1965**, the then South Vietnamese Prime Minister, Air Vice-Marshal Nguyen Cao Ky, made, what was for the Americans on the eve of their first major offensive against the Viet Cong, the somewhat embarrassing statement that the infamous Adolf Hitler was one of his heroes. This coupled with the knowledge that South Vietnamese politics were known to be extremely corrupt, raised the obvious question of why the Americans had ever chosen to support them. What it did show was that her dislike and mistrust of anything relating to communism was so strong, that she was prepared to do anything and everything within her power to prevent it from spreading, no matter where in the world that might be.

On **28 July 1965**, President Johnson announces that the number of United States troops will be increased to 125,000 meaning that monthly draft calls increased from 17,000 to 35,000.

By **August** of that year, the 9th MEB had become the 3rd Marine Amphibious Force, comprised of four Marine regiments, each consisting of three battalions. This was increased further when in **December** they were joined by two more battalions from the 1st Marines.

On **5 August 1965**, the Viet Cong continue their tactic of attacking large businesses when they target a large Esso storage facility near Da Nang. This results in America losing two million gallons of much-needed fuel, which was almost 40 per cent of its entire supply.

Things really begin to heat up on **7 August 1965**, when China threatens that it might send in troops to fight alongside the North Vietnamese and Viet Cong forces. The threat, as is best known, never comes to fruition.

Operation Starlite or the Battle of Van Tuong, as it was also known, took place between **18** and **24 August 1965**, and was the first major offensive of regimental size action carried out by a purely United States unit, during the Vietnam War. It was a pre-emptive strike against a large Viet Cong force of some 1,500 men who were planning an attack on the Chu Lai air base, which had quickly become an important American military stronghold operated by the United States Marine Corps.

The operation became a combined arms assault and included troops on the ground, Marines being deployed by helicopter insertion, and an amphibious landing on the coastline of Van Tuong, whilst the USS *Galveston* and *Cabildo* provided naval gunfire support. At the end of the day both sides claimed the battle as a victory although, if the body count was anything to go by, it was hard to see how that could possibly be. The Viet Cong lost 614 of their men, against America's 45. What had turned this particular battle in the Americans favour was their superior fire power which they were able to throw at their enemy, from all directions. This had caused the Viet Cong to stand and fight face-to-face in a battle that the Americans had instigated and not them, meaning that it wasn't fought on their terms. In essence they had been trapped and forced to fight in a manner that was alien to them.

Operation Starlite saw the shift in American strategy in Vietnam, from the defending of enclaves, to the more robust and proactive style of search and destroy. This changed America's role in Vietnam from being the 'military advisors', only there to support the South Vietnamese, to the main fighting machine taking on the Viet Cong and the North Vietnamese forces. General William Westmoreland and the United States defence establishment were not in total agreement on this point, but the General, who was the main protagonist pushing the new search and destroy tactics, finally won the day. Whether it was the right thing to do, and whether it was in the best interests of America, is another question.

Between **7** and **10 September 1965**, a combination of United States and South Vietnamese troops begin Operation Piranha, in an attempt to destroy the remainder of the 1st Regiment of the Viet Cong, following on from Operation Starlite. The United States military authorities claimed that 200 enemy were killed during the attack on a Viet Cong stronghold. The reality was that most of the enemy they discovered in the stronghold were those who had been wounded during Operation Starlite.

On **11 September 1965**, the US 1st Cavalry Division (Airmobile) begins to land at Quy Nhon. This brings the total strength of American troops in Vietnam to almost 125,000.

The last of the 1st Cavalry Division arrived at An Khe on **21 September 1965**, and the following month saw the arrival of the entire 1st Infantry Division, often referred to in American military parlance as 'The Big Red One'.

During the period of **23** to the **29 September 1965**, three communist agents are executed by South Vietnamese authorities in Da Nang. The executions are carried out at night, so that they cannot be so easily recorded by foreign journalists and photographers. North Vietnamese authorities in Hanoi retaliated by announcing that they had executed two American prisoners, who had been held since 1963, as 'war criminals'. This would suggest that the men concerned would have been downed United States pilots.

By **October 1965**, American Special Forces in the shape of the Green Berets, numbered 1828. Since 1961, the Special Forces community had been involved in organising what was called the Civilian Irregular Defense Group program (CIDG). These camps were initially manned by people from ethnic minority regions of the country, particularly the Montagnard tribesmen. In October 1965, the number who had trained up as 'cidgees' had reached 30,400 men.

On **15 October 1965**, David J. Millar, who was a relief programme volunteer in America, and a pacifist, became the first war protester to burn his draft card in public in the United States, which is an offence. He was arrested three days later in Hooksett, New Hampshire, by the FBI. He was prosecuted, found guilty and sent to prison.

On **16 October 1965**, a two-day demonstration against the war in Vietnam begins outside the American Embassy in London. This is mirrored in numerous other European cities, including Rome, Brussels and Stockholm, as well as in most major cities of the United States.

In **December 1965**, the 3rd Brigade, 25th Infantry Division, began arriving in Vietnam, along with complete support services including medical personnel, helicopter and fixed-wing capabilities, engineers and artillery units.

When taking into account all the events which took place throughout 1965, it becomes apparent how quickly the war developed during that time. The Vietnam of February 1965 was very different from the Vietnam of October that same year. It is quite staggering to think that during that relatively short period of time, Vietnam had changed from being a place where troops could have family flown out to visit them, to being somewhere young men didn't even want to go to, let alone have family over to visit.

The year 1965 had seen Vietnam change from being a country in which the US had 23,000 military advisors stationed, who were there for no other purpose than to support the sovereign nation of South Vietnam, to being a country where the US actually led the conflict with 150,000 troops there.

Despite the fact that they had greatly increased the number of men sent out to Vietnam, America made two attempts at bringing an end to the war, but the North Vietnamese had turned these opportunities down flat. They weren't even prepared to sit down and have any kind of discussion.

With all the activity across North Vietnam, and the Pathet Lao occupying parts of Laos, another possible explanation for the disappearance of flight F-BELV came to mind. Maybe the North Vietnamese, or the Pathet Lao fighters, believed that the aircraft had seen something on the ground, such as a large movement of their forces in preparation for a surprise attack. Rather than run the risk of F-BELV reporting the co-ordinates of what they had seen, they were shot down.

Chapter 13

The other nine Stratoliners

As mentioned earlier, only ten Boeing 307 Stratoliners were ever built. This was no reflection of the aircraft's capabilities or reliability, but due to the outbreak of the war, Boeing had to change their production to cater for military aircraft, and by the time the war was over aircraft design had moved on.

Each aircraft was allocated a construction number and a name, apart from the first of them which was never allocated a name.

The first Stratoliner had a construction number of **1994**, but at the time of its crash it had not been allocated a name. The crash occurred at Alder, Washington on 18 March 1939, killing all ten people on board.

Witnesses to the crash described how the aircraft appeared suddenly from out of the clouds, as the noise of its engines momentarily could not be heard, before greatly speeding up as it plunged to earth in an uncontrolled spin. During its rapid descent the tail section broke away. It hit the ground with such impact that there could never have been any survivors.

The Stratoliner was the first four-engine transport aircraft to also be equipped with passenger cabins and facilities, for high altitude flying at 20,000 feet or above. It could carry a maximum of thirty-three passengers by day, or twenty-five in luxurious accommodation during night flights, and the aircraft could operate just as effectively with a crew of either four or five.

This was not the most auspicious start that a newly-designed aircraft could have made.

One of its innovations was a 'super charged' cabin, which could provide 'sea level' air pressure whilst flying at 20,000 feet. It had a sealed cabin which had air pumped into it, allowing the air pressure to be maintained.

It had a wingspan of 107 feet and was 74 feet in length, with an overall height of just over 20 feet.

The second of the ten Stratoliners had the construction number **1995** and had the name 'Clipper Rainbow'. It was originally sold to Pan American airlines, which for years was better known as Pan Am. During the Second World War it was commandeered by the United States Air Force, but flown for them by a Pan Am crew. After the war it was returned to civilian use and in 1948 Pan Am sold it to a company in Ecuador who owned it for nine years before selling it on to Aigle Azur Extreme Orient, who were based in Saigon. In 1960 they leased the aircraft to Air Laos.

On 22 May 1961, whilst still leased to Air Laos, it was attempting to land at Tan Son Nhat Airport in Saigon, on only three engines. It was a heavy landing and although there were no injuries or fatalities to any of those on board, the aircraft was so badly damaged that it never flew again. Instead it was used for spare parts for other Stratoliners based in Vietnam.

Next came **1996** which had the name 'Comanche'. It was initially sold to Trans World Airlines, which was more commonly referred to as simply, TWA. During the war it saw service with the US Air Force as a C-75.

After the war it went back in to civilian use and like Clipper Rainbow, it was sold to Aigle Azur Extreme Orient who, in turn, leased it to Air Laos and eventually sold on to Compagnie Internationale de Transports Civil Aériens, who leased it to the International

Commission for Supervision and Control, where it became flight F-BELV, and was lost in Indochina during the Vietnam War.

Then came **1997**, or 'Flying Penthouse', which was the aircraft that the well-known American philanthropist, Howard Hughes, purchased. He modified it to be used as VIP transport for a round-the-world flying attempt, which he never made due to the outbreak of the Second World War. It had a dining table and chairs, its own bar, and sleeping accommodation. It really was the epitome of wealth and extravagance. He sold it in 1948 to a Texas hotelier, and the following year it was sold to American oil tycoon, Glenn McCarthy. In 1965, whilst at Broward International Airport, Fort Lauderdale, it was damaged in a storm.

In the early 2000s it was 'rebuilt' as a boathouse called the 'Cosmic Muffin'.

The only surviving Boeing Model 307 Stratoliner is NC19903, which was operated by Pan Am airways, and is now preserved at the Smithsonian National Air and Space Museum in Fairfax County, Virginia. On its way to the Smithsonian on 29 March 2002, it had to ditch in Elliot Bay in Seattle, Washington. Thankfully, it was restored to its former glory.

Construction number **1998** had the name of 'Cherokee' and was originally sold to Trans World Airlines as a passenger aircraft. During the Second World War it was commandeered for military purposes, and changed to a C-75. After the war it was returned to civilian use and leased to Aigle Azure and later sold to Compagnie Internationale de Transports Civil Aériens, whose headquarters were situated in Paris. During the Vietnam War it was leased to the International Commission for Supervision and Control for use in Indochina, where it was still working in 1973.

The **1999** Model 307 Stratoliner had the name of 'Zuni' and the same history as 'Cherokee'.

The **2000** was given the name 'Apache' and had a similar history to both the 1998 and 1999, but additionally, during the Vietnam

War, it was working throughout Indochina. Upon landing at Luang-Prabang Airport in Laos, and in circumstances which were unclear, it accidentally struck a C-47 aircraft. There were no injuries, but the Stratoliner 307 was damaged beyond repair.

The **2001** was another of the Stratoliners given an Indian name, 'Navajo'. It was one of the aircraft which was originally sold to Trans World Airlines, but during the Second World War it was used as a C-75 aircraft. After the war it returned to civilian use and was eventually sold to Aigle Azure, who in turn leased the aircraft to Airnautic. It crashed at Monte Renoso, in Corsica, on 29 December 1962, killing all twenty-five people on board.

The **2002** had the name of 'Clipper Comet' and was originally purchased by Pan Am Airways in America, who later sold it to Aerovias Ecuatorianas of Quito, Ecuador, in 1950. Between 1955 and 1957 it was operated by Quaker City Airways in the United States. In 1958 it had additional fuel tanks attached to provide it with a greater flying range. Whilst it was undergoing a test run with its added fuel tanks, it crashed 15 miles west of Madras, Oregon. All of the crew escaped uninjured, but the aircraft was completely destroyed by fire.

The **2003** was named the 'Clipper Flying Cloud'. It was initially owned by Pan Am Airlines, who purchased the aircraft on 20 March 1940, at Brownsville, Texas. During the Second World War it was used by the Army Air Transport Command on South American routes to and from the United States. On 1 November 1948, it was sold to Airline Training Incorporated of Homestead, Florida, which would be its home for the next five years. On 11 December 1953, it was purchased by the Haitian Army Air Corps, for use as the personal transport of the country's President, Francois 'Papa Doc' Duvalier.

On 15 September 1959, it returned to the United States when it was purchased by the Flight Investment Corporation of Dallas, Texas, and registered as N9307R. On 12 November 1962, it was bought by

Ewell Nold Jr., of South Houston, Texas. It later flew for Arkansas Air Freight Incorporated until 23 November 1965, when it was purchased by Inter-American, who were based in Derby, Kansas, who in turn sold it to Aviation Specialities Company from Mesa, Arizona, on 28 May 1969.

On 28 March 2002, it was on its final flight to the Smithsonian National Air and Space Museum's new Steven F. Udvar-Hazy Center at Washington Dulles International Airport, Virginia, when it was ditched in Seattle's Elliot Bay, due to an error over the amount of fuel the aircraft was carrying. It was believed there was enough fuel for two hours of flying, when in fact there was only enough for just forty-five minutes.

Luckily the aircraft's four-man crew received only minor injuries in the ditching manoeuvre. The stricken aircraft was lifted intact from the river the following day. The makers of the aircraft set about restoring it to flight-worthy condition and on 13 June 2003, the restoration was complete. It is now on display at the Smithsonian at Dulles.

It is fair to say that the 'Clipper Flying Cloud' was one aircraft which certainly had an eventful existence.

Chapter 14

James Sylvester Byrne

James Sylvester Byrne was born in Dublin in 1929, he was one of four children and the only son born to Thomas and Mary Byrne. He was a bit of a nomad and left home at a relatively young age and enlisted in the Merchant Navy, before settling in Canada and joining the army in time to take part in the Korean War.

James Sylvester Byrne had a stepson by the name of Donald J. Byrne. He is a man I have never met, but as we are both related to James, I suppose that gives us a family connection. We do have one thing in common though, James also went by the name of Jim, whilst Donald uses the shortened version of his name, Don, and as for myself, I am more often than not referred to as Steve, rather than what my mother always called me, especially when I was in any kind of trouble, Stephen.

I had known of Donald's existence going back many years, but I only managed to trace him back in the middle of 2014, when the idea to write this book first came to mind. He had some interesting observations to make and told me about a meeting he had in the early part of 2014, when he was contacted out of the blue by a guy from America. This man flew to Canada and met Donald for lunch. He told Donald that he was of the opinion that James was not in Indochina as just an ordinary rotated in member of the International Commission for Supervision and Control, but that he was there in an official intelligence capacity and that the North Vietnamese had become aware of this, and so intentionally shot down flight F-BELV.

In some respects this makes perfect sense and in others it doesn't, but I will return to that shortly.

Donald would not say how the meeting came about, what the man's name was or what if any agency he worked for. I didn't push the point, as I understood and respected his reasons for not elaborating any further on the matter. This anonymous American also added that intelligence was being shared between Canada and the United States.

The comments about James working in 'intelligence' made perfect sense to Donald as, prior to the Vietnam War, James had worked as a Military attaché in many 'Cold War' hot spots, including Prague, Czechoslovakia, in July 1950, where his security level was raised to 'Top Secret'.

When describing James, Donald said,

> 'I have told many people that Jim knew more about political science than any university professor I have ever met. He looked at the bigger picture. His education in this field was self-taught, and his political acumen was amazing.' Donald continued, 'I took Jim's surname to honour him following his death, and I am proud to say that I am the stepson of Sergeant James Sylvester Byrne. I know prior to his death Jim was working in the orphanages in Saigon, as he had also done during our stay in Rome, Italy during 1961 and 1962. During our stay in Rome, Jim and his friends from the Canadian Embassy would quite often go to the orphanages and drive the kids around on a Saturday.'

It was clear from reading what Donald had written about his stepfather, how strongly he felt about him and how close their relationship had been.

I was 10 years of age at the time of Jim's death on October 18, 1965. I saw the local priest entering our home as I was playing with a friend. I immediately went home and knew something was very wrong when I heard my mother crying.

Although he doesn't mention it, such news would have been very painful for Donald, who was just a 10-year-old child at the time. One minute his life would have been no more complicated than playing with a friend in the street, and then the next thing he knew, the man who had become his father suddenly disappeared, on an aircraft in a part of the world which he had possibly never even heard of, presumed dead. It must have been a very surreal experience for Donald, with his initial feeling of disbelief giving way to a begrudging acceptance of what had happened, to an expectation that James would walk through the front door of their home, hoping that it would all just be a bad dream. But the reality was the complete opposite. The death of a loved one for a child always has a different feeling to it. At that age life is all about playing and having a good time, and parents are just that, your parents. They look after you, tell you what you have to do and when you have to do it, whilst making life nice and comfortable. They are always just there for you, and you have no perception that one day they no longer will be.

One final note from Donald's memories of James:

I remember Jim telling me that when he was 13 years of age, and living in Dublin, he went home one day and told his father, Thomas Byrne, that he had enlisted in the British Navy. On hearing what James had said, he proceeded in chasing him out of the house. He apparently did not return until he was 18 years of age, following three trips around the world. I believe these trips provided him with an excellent education and were also the very building blocks which helped provide him with his knowledge of world affairs and politics.

James's father, Thomas Byrne, was a veteran of the First World War, having first arrived in Egypt on 21 February 1915. He began his military service as Private 2600 serving with the Royal Irish Rifles Regiment before later transferring to the Cheshire Regiment as Private 78004, and later serving as Private 27850 in the Cambridgeshire Regiment. Finally, he was demobbed on 18 March 1919.

Maybe it was because he had been a soldier that Thomas Byrne was annoyed with James for joining the navy.

Returning to the claim that flight F-BELV was intentionally shot down by the North Vietnamese. The factor which didn't make sense was that if the North Vietnamese actually did believe James Sylvester Byrne to be an intelligence officer working for the Canadian military, who in turn were passing intelligence provided by him over to their American counterparts, then surely there would have been some very useful political propaganda to have been gained from not interfering with flight F-BELV. Instead they could have let it land in Hanoi, arrested James Sylvester Byrne, and had a showcase trial which would have deeply embarrassed both the American and Canadian governments, especially if the North Vietnamese had evidence to back up such allegations.

The other side of the argument could be that if the North Vietnamese authorities had shot down flight F-BELV, not only would they have rid themselves of an immediate threat to their national security, but they could then have quite easily covered up any of the subsequent searches undertaken to locate the downed aircraft to ensure that its wreckage was never recovered by anyone other than themselves.

Whilst looking through James Byrne's army service record I came across a number of letters relating to the estate of James Byrne, many of which were in relation to the payment of insurance claims connected directly to his death. Although these letters have no connection to the disappearance of flight F-BELV, they are, I believe, still relevant to the overall story, as highlighting the importance for the next of kin, and how the Canadian authorities pushed for the awarding of 'presumption of death certificates' early on in the proceedings, when they knew that the chances of anyone from flight F-BELV ever being found alive were extremely low. Despite the fact that, understandably, the next of kin of all of those on board held on to the faint hope and belief that their loved ones were still alive, due to no wreckage having been found, the reality was that they were deceased and the Canadian authorities knew this so went about doing the best they could for the families of the three Canadian nationals involved.

The first of these letters was sent from the Canadian Forces Headquarters in Ottawa, to the Under Secretary of State for External Affairs, and was dated 11 May 1967. The content of the letter concerned the insurance claim appertaining to James Byrne.

A few things drew my attention. The letter pointed out that although James Byrne's wife had a son from a previous marriage, as James 'had not taken any steps to legally adopt the child, Donald Joseph O'Connor, it is therefore considered that the tutorship of this child is of no real concern to this claim'. This seemed somewhat harsh in the circumstances, and was more than likely something which he had always intended to do, but simply had not got round to doing. He certainly treated him like his own son.

The letter went on to mention James' mother, Mary Byrne, and two of his sisters, but also included, 'For personal reasons Mrs Byrne would prefer not to make any direct approach to these people at this time, unless it is considered really necessary to obtain birth and death certificates before payment could be made.' I have absolutely no knowledge of the relationship between James' wife and his mother, but it still seems a very strange statement to make. I can only assume that, for some reason or other, they didn't get on with each other.

A further comment in the letter states that 'it is not believed that he had any other brothers or sisters.' My mother was James's elder half-sister.

Another letter addressed to the Under Secretary of State for External Affairs, at the Department of External Affairs, in Ottawa, Ontario, was dated 23 February 1968. It concerned the requested release forms by 'Les Experts Reunis S.A.', which had been prepared in both English and French and had been signed individually by the next of kin, James Byrne and Vernon J. Perkin.

On the second page of the letter were a number of names and addresses, two of them were Mrs Bridget McCarthy, of 38 Thistle Grove, Welwyn Garden City, Hertfordshire, and Mrs Bernadette Strickland, of 48 Bourne Road, Gravesend, Kent. These were the details of two of James' sisters, my aunties. Having spoken to Bernadette Strickland many years back about James Byrne, I remember her saying that when he died, all such payments understandably went to his widow and that she definitely did not receive any monies from any insurance pay-outs.

James' mother, and my grandmother, Mary Byrne, are also among the names mentioned on the correspondence, but somewhat surprisingly my mother, Angela Wynn, is not one of the names mentioned. Maybe this is to do with the fact that she was his half-sister, they had the same mother but different fathers.

An earlier letter had been sent to Sheila Byrne, dated 18 January 1968, and sent by a Captain A.O. Solomon, on behalf of the Chief of the Defence Staff, informing her that James' two sisters and his mother had been contacted by letter, informing them that it was intended that the full insurance payment of 82,000 francs from the French insurance company, 'Compagnie d'assurances maritimes, aériennes et terrestres', would be paid directly to her. The letter sent to James's mother, Mrs Mary Byrne, explaining the above, was dated

10 January 1968, and was received by her five days later. Neither Mary nor James' two sisters made any counter-claim against the French insurance company and all of the monies were sent, uncontested, to Mrs Shelia Byrne.

The following is a letter sent to James' wife, Shelia, from the National Defence Headquarters in Ottawa, and dated April 1973. At the time Mrs Byrne was living in Aylmer, just outside the town of Ottawa.

Dear Mrs Byrne,

The Under-Secretary of State for External Affairs has contacted this department concerning the disappearance in 1965 of the aircraft carrying your husband, Sergeant James Sylvester Byrne, as well as two other Canadians. I thought you may wish to be informed about recent happenings in this matter.

During his visit to Hanoi on March 18 the Secretary of State for External Affairs, the Honourable Mitchell Sharp, raised the matter with the Foreign Minister of the Democratic Republic of Vietnam, Mr Nguyen Duy Trinh. Although the enquiry elicited no new information, Mr Trinh assured Mr Sharp that a further enquiry would be undertaken.

Regrettably, nothing of a positive nature has been ascertained concerning your husband's disappearance, however, you may be sure that both departments will continue to seek information which may help to shed light on this mysterious and distressing incident.

You will be informed of any new developments as soon as they are known.

Yours sincerely
J A Dextraze
General
Chief of the Defence Staff.

James Sylvester Byrne was my uncle, a man who I never met. He was my late mother's younger half-brother, who was born in Dublin on 17 April 1929, but it was as if his destiny had already determined that he would spend most of his life far away from his country of birth. He enlisted in the Canadian army on 21 August 1950, when he was 21 years of age. Prior to this he had worked as a waiter and a bartender in London between 1943 and 1944. Between 1944 and 1947 he worked as a deckhand and steward in the Merchant Navy. From 1947 to 1949 he became a tour organiser to Italy, and in the first half of 1950 he worked as a batman at the Royal Canadian Armed Forces Staff College.

On his enlistment papers James wrote that his interests were darts, swimming, dancing and boxing.

So even before becoming a Canadian soldier he had spent many years away from home. My mother recalls that when he did return home from whatever exotic ports he had been visiting, he usually had presents of some kind for everyone.

Having settled in Canada he acquired himself a chauffeur's licence, issued in 1962, number 903093. A man of many talents, and obviously someone who could turn his hand to most things in an effort to earn a living.

He began his military career in the Canadian army as a Private First Class. On 2 October 1951, he was appointed as an Acting Corporal. Just two months later on 30 December 1951, he was confirmed in the rank of Corporal. He was then appointed as Acting Sergeant on 6 May 1952, and that of Temporary Sergeant on 5 August 1952.

His army service record includes a personal planning sheet dated 20 July 1954, in which he indicates his options for his next posting as either Vancouver or Toronto, which he was due to take up on 16 July 1955. At the time, he was stationed overseas in Tokyo, Japan and the Far East, where he had served, along with time spent in Korea between 22 April 1951 and June 1955. As he came to the end of his tour of duty, he applied for extended leave and permission to be allowed to travel outside of Canada, specifically to England, Ireland, France, Belgium and Italy, in continental Europe. Surprisingly enough he also had to seek permission to wear civilian clothes whilst abroad on leave.

Despite the fact that James Byrne had enlisted in the Canadian army in 1950, he didn't apply to become a Canadian citizen until 18 February 1955, almost five years later. His application was approved and his certificate of Canadian citizenship was sent to his commanding officer, Captain F.A. Leger, Deputy Judge Advocate, Mission for Far East, Vancouver, Canada, with a covering letter dated 22 March 1955.

In a confidential report written about him by a Captain J.L. Davies and Major F.N. Clifford and signed 13 May 1955, were the following comments,

> Leadership characteristics and qualities becoming an officer are at all times evident. Sgt Byrne is soldiery in appearance, moderate in habits and conducts himself in an exemplary manner continuously. His recommendation for immediate promotion is endorsed and upon furthering his education Byrne is considered potential Officer material.

It is somewhat sad to think that with a recommendation as glowing and forthright as that, ten years later at the time of his death, he had not been promoted to the rank of officer.

In 1958 he was temporarily sent to serve at Fort Churchill in Manitoba, which had a chequered history, being opened and closed on more than one occasion. It was a location which was also used by United States forces, and it was an extremely cold region, the coldest temperature ever recorded there being -50.1°C. The following year, in 1959, he was once again given a temporary duty working out of Whitehorse, which is the capital of northwest Canada's Yukon territory, and is also known as Canada's wilderness city.

Between June 1959 and April 1960 he served in Prague, in what was then the country of Czechoslovakia. In May 1962, when he was looking at future postings, he certainly included some varied choices. His first choice was Army Headquarters in Ottawa. His second was a posting to somewhere in the British Columbia area. After that he requested a tour with the Egyptian Expeditionary Force in either Gaza or the Congo, and then as another option he added in a tour with the Brigade Group in Germany.

A report dated 29 May 1962, written by his commanding officer, Captain W.D. Milne, of the Royal Canadian Army Service Corps Personnel department, was glowing in its praise for James Byrne:

> Sgt Byrne is employed as my clerk. As I am the only officer here and he the only other soldier, he does nearly all my clerical work, assists me in my reports and is in command in my absence.
>
> I consider myself fortunate in having had Sgt Byrne as my clerk for the past 20 months. He is punctual, hardworking, loyal and cheerful. His appearance is extremely neat both in uniform and in plain clothes.
>
> He has had to perform a number of jobs, not normally given to an NCO; some of these require physical work, whilst others demand considerable tact and discretion. This NCO was able to do them to my entire satisfaction. I would like to read his compliments which I received on behalf of Sgt Byrne, from my many colleagues who deal with him; they said to me that he was 'a real soldier'.
>
> He certainly gives the impression of being a competent and conscientious NCO. He is quick to grasp the details and requirements of all tasks that he is set to undertake,

and complete it quickly and with accuracy. He is polite and well-spoken and is popular with all members of the staff.

Although circumstances do not allow me to actually judge his instructional ability, I reckon that Sgt Byrne would, given the proper training, make a good instructor. Any Corps courses would enable this NCO to get ahead, especially one which demands qualities of leadership which he possesses to a noticeable degree.

Sgt Byrne has proved himself to be an extremely valuable member of the Personnel department, Royal Canadian Army Service Corps.

His previous report which covered the period 19 September 1960 to 1 June 1961, had been similarly glowing in its praise of James. It was written by the same officer who at the time had only been his commanding officer for a matter of months, so although it was a good report, he probably wasn't marked as highly as he could and should have been.

On 24 June 1963, James Byrne was stationed at Camp Petawawa in Ontario, where he was an Admin Clerk, Group 3, and part of the Headquarters Training Company 'D', Personnel, Royal Canadian Army Service Corps.

The previous day, just before midnight, he was asleep in the top level of a bunk bed, when he rolled over, fell out on to the floor some 4 feet below, and hurt his shoulder. The following morning he reported the incident to the medical officer, because when he woke up he was in a considerable amount of pain. An X-ray of his right shoulder revealed that there was no fracture or break, but he remained in some discomfort for a number of days and was therefore placed on light duties, as movement of the arm was still somewhat restricted.

On 8 October 1965, whilst stationed with the Canadian Delegation of the International Commission for Supervision and Control, he was interviewed about his next posting on his return to Canada, after he had completed his stint with the ICSC. He completed and submitted an advance planning sheet which allowed him to indicate three preferences whilst being interviewed by a Major C.W. Turton.

The form included the information that he was a Sergeant (SB 801786) in the Royal Canadian Army Service Corps as an administrative clerk, and had been stationed in Vietnam since arriving there at 1310 hours on 16 July 1965, when he touched down in Saigon, having travelled first class on a Canadian Pacific Airlines commercial flight from Vancouver. The journey had taken almost two days, having left Vancouver on 14 July before arriving in Hong Kong the following day, where he stayed overnight at the Miramar Hotel in Kowloon. His journey continued the following day when he took a four-hour flight to Saigon.

He was a married man, and his wife, Shelia E. Byrne, lived in the town of Aylmer in the county of Elgin in southern Ontario, where they owned a house. Shelia had a son Donald, who James Sylvester Byrne happily took on as his own.

Two of the three options he had chosen were to be sent to the Canadian Forces Headquarters, which was situated in Ontario. His other choice was to go to work at Project Emergency Army Signals Establishment (EASE), which was situated in the rural community of Carp, Ontario.

His reason for requesting one of these three postings was: 'I own a home in the Ottawa area. Also my son has been an honour student for the past three years in a French school and I feel that a change now would be detrimental to his education.'

At the time, his stepson Donald was 11 years of age.

Major Turton, who had completed the form, wrote the following remarks. 'While Sgt Byrne's reasons are personal, I nevertheless concur in his request, particularly in view of his son's future education. Sgt Byrne is an outstanding reliable NCO.'

The reference to EASE refers to the 'Diefenbunker', which today is a former Canadian military facility. The name is derived from the former Canadian Prime Minister, John Diefenbaker, who in 1959 authorised the building of up to fifty such bunkers, which were intended as Emergency Government Headquarters at the height of the Cold War, when there was a genuine belief that Russia intended to fire intercontinental ballistic missiles at Canada.

Work on the Diefenbunker was completed in 1962, and it could accommodate up to 565 people. It consisted of four levels, all of which were underground. It included a broadcasting studio, and a large vault on its lowest level to hold the Bank of Canada's gold reserves.

On 10 December 1965, an ad-hoc committee made up of three members of the ICSC delivered their report into the investigation they had carried out regarding the loss of flight F-BELV.

The members of that committee were:

(1) Lieutenant-Colonel N.A. Dave – Indian Delegation Chairman.
(2) Colonel M. Bugaj – Polish Delegation – Member.
(3) Major C.W. Turton – Canadian Delegation – Member.

Major Turton left Vietnam on 24 November 1965, having finished his tour of duty with the Commission and returned to Canada having been posted to other duties. His position on the ad-hoc committee was taken by his replacement, Squadron Leader Y.J. Lavigne of the Canadian delegation, who arrived in Vietnam on 25 November 1965.

The ad-hoc committee's first meeting took place on 25 October 1965 in Saigon. Their Mandate was that it should investigate and report upon the disappearance of the ICSC aircraft F-BELV, and all relevant matters pertaining to its disappearance. It was specifically required to look into the following points:

(1) The air worthiness of aircraft F-BELV.
(2) The qualifications and health of the aircraft's crew.
(3) The safety aids on board the aircraft.
(4) The survival equipment on board the aircraft.
(5) The state of the aircraft's wireless equipment.
(6) All available aircraft flight logs.
(7) Details of the contract with CITCA of Paris.
(8) Servicing and fuel load.
(9) Flight plan, including clearances, contacts and stops.
(10) Times of departures and arrivals of each stop.
(11) Passenger and Freight manifests, along with payload.
(12) Number of diplomatic mail bags.
(13) All messages from aircraft and Hanoi Control Tower.
(14) Weather information.
(15) What search and rescue operations were carried out.
(16) Circumstances under which F-BELV disappeared.

The inquiry report included the following information.

Before leaving Saigon for Vientiane, the ad-hoc committee's chairman met the manager of CITCA, Mr Albre, who promised that all the available information concerning flight F-BELV that his company had would be given to the ad-hoc committee. The committee's secretary, Major J.G. Walkay, was directed to visit CITCA to collect this information and bring it with him to Vientiane on 26 October 1965.

On his arrival at Vientiane, Major Walkay met with the other committee members who were present to inform them that he had visited CITCA as requested, but none of the information which had been promised was made available to him. He had, however, been informed by the company that it would be forthcoming in due course.

On 27 October 1965, the members of the ad-hoc committee, along with members of the ICSC from both the Vientiane and Saigon offices, met to discuss the ad-hoc committee's mandate concerning their inquiry in to the disappearance of flight F-BELV.

After their meeting at Vientiane, the ad-hoc committee moved on to Hanoi where they arrived on 28 October 1965, and met with members of the ICSC who were given a questionnaire in relation to the ad-hoc committee's inquiry. They also interviewed the following members of the Hanoi branch of the ICSC, in an attempt to discover as much information about the disappearance of flight F-BELV as possible.

(1) Mr A.W.B. Vaz, Chairman of the Hanoi branch of ICSC.

(2) Lieutenant-Colonel A. Guha, Station Commander.

(3) Lieutenant-Colonel C. Sroka, Polish representative.

(4) Major H.T. Haney, Canadian representative.

(5) Major M.S. Kadyan, Team Officer.

(6) Captain G. Selladurai, Signal Officer.

(7) Mr D. Ky, Assistant at the ICSC Hanoi.

The ad-hoc committee was due to submit its report to the Secretary General of the ICSC in Laos by 6 November 1965, but as it had been held up in Hanoi until 5 November 1965, it had been arranged for them to briefly meet with staff from the ICSC in Cambodia at the airport at Phnom Penh, whilst on their way back to Saigon. Having arrived there they interviewed members of the OC Signal Company and the Incharge Movement Control Detachment of the ICSC in Vietnam.

No response had been received from CITCA, so the ad-hoc committee managed to establish through other official sources that F-BELV had in fact been an airworthy aircraft, that all members of the crew were competent and professional, and that the wireless set had been in good working order up until 1520 hours on 18 October 1965.

It is worth noting at this stage that the ad-hoc committee members flew from Vientiane to Hanoi, along the exact same route and flight path taken by flight F-BELV, and that neither did they see any ground wreckage that could have been from the missing aircraft, nor did they encounter any 'aggression' from either the ground or other aircraft.

After having conducted all of their inquiries, the ad-hoc committee produced its report in to the disappearance of flight F-BELV.

The aircraft was not a commercial one, but an authorised chartered flight of the ICSC, on route from Saigon to Hanoi, via Phnom Penh and Vientiane. It had been scheduled by the ICSC in accordance with the contract between CITCA in Saigon, with the ICSC in Vietnam. The report also included the original departure time from Saigon, along with the arrival and departure times from both Phnom Penh and Vientiane. It was due to land at Hanoi at 1658 hours, but it never arrived.

The flight path between Vientiane and Hanoi included flying over Muong Sen, then Phu Ly, and from there direct to Gia Lam Airport in Hanoi. The altitude of the flight was to be at 3600 metres which would have made the aircraft clearly visible form the ground.

The following is the report's 'Synoptic Analysis'.

At 0800 hours, local time 18 Oct 65, a High Pressure area was centred at Latitude 28N Longitude 115E, giving an east-southeasterly flow of moist air over the entire surface of LAOS and the DRVN along the flight route. The wind at altitude was reported to be 045 true at 15 knots. CLOUDS AND WEATHER: As per forecast, the clouds along the route were to consist of 7/8 heavy cumulus over the 'chaine annamitique' based at 2500 feet above ground with light turbulence in cloud. This reducing to 5/8 heavy cumulus to the west and the east of the mountain range.

The actual weather at VIENTIANE Airport at the time
of departure was 1/8 cumulus based at 2500 feet above
ground and surface wind was 045 at 6 knots.

In essence, this part of the report explained that the weather was normal
for the time of year, and that with clear blue skies there was nothing
out of the ordinary which could have possibly been responsible for
bringing down or causing the crash of F-BELV.

The report then went on to look at the geographical and climatic
conditions of the areas that flight F-BELV was due to have flown
over, 185 miles of which included the Annamite mountain range. This
distance would have taken one hour and fifteen minutes to fly at the
speed the aircraft was flying at, 165 nautical miles per hour. Vientiane
is at an altitude of 559 feet above sea level, but within 25 nautical miles
eastwards of that point, heading across Laos towards North Vietnam,
the terrain rises sharply 3,500 feet and averages between 4,000 to
5,000 feet in elevation until latitude 20N, with sharp peaks as high
as 8,900 feet near the Laotian/North Vietnamese border. This is a
mountainous region with deep ravines, which is completely covered
with tropical rain forests and trees that average between 70 to 100 feet
in height, below which is a thick jungle undergrowth. The area is not
densely populated, and those who do live there are mainly migrant
Miao tribesmen and contact with them is restricted to jungle tracks
which mainly run in a north/south direction alongside streams and in
the valleys. The rainfall in this region is heaviest during the months
of September and October.

The route being followed by F-BELV was a scheduled and
approved flight which took place on a weekly basis, and twice
weekly every other week. But nothing was taken for granted and it
had become customary for the crews who flew the ICSC members
on these journeys to contact the control tower at Gia Lam Airport,
soon after leaving Vientiane. They did this for three reasons, firstly to

obtain permission and provide an estimated time of arrival to land in Hanoi, secondly to inform them at what time they would be crossing the border from Laos in to North Vietnamese air space, and thirdly what route they would be taking between the border with Laos and Hanoi. This also included the anticipated time they expected to be flying over Phu Ly.

All four members of the crew were French:

(1) Captain Domerque – Pilot.
(2) Mr Lemee – Radio Officer.
(3) Mr Ropers – Engineer Officer.
(4) Mr Gustin – Steward.

All of the above worked for and were employed by CITCA, whose headquarters in Vietnam were in Saigon, but they were a Paris-based company in France. The following five individuals were all part of the Indian delegation that was attached to the ICSC, all of whom were on the aircraft from Saigon.

(1) Mr S.L. Bhalla.
(2) Captain C.K. Bhattacharjee.
(3) Mr Jagdish Prasad.
(4) Mr Bhola Singh.
(5) Mr M.R. Ramani.

The next three individuals were those from the Canadian delegation who were attached to the ICSC. The first two were on the flight from Saigon, whilst the third individual only joined the flight at Vientiane.

(1) Sergeant James Sylvester Byrne.
(2) Corporal Vernon J. Perkin.
(3) Mr J.D. Turner (Diplomat).

The report also looked at the aircraft's total payload, which took into account all personal luggage, diplomatic mail bags, cargo, and even the combined weight of the nine passengers. The total weight of all of the above came to 1234 kilograms whilst the aircraft's payload for the flight was 2800 kilograms, so it was clear to see that in no way was F-BELV overloaded. The weight of the crew and the 1,600 gallons of fuel in the aircraft's petrol tanks is not something that is factored in to the equation.

An interesting aspect of the report is the comments that are included in relation to the airworthiness of F-BELV. Despite two requests made by the ad-hoc committee to have sight of the certificate of airworthiness for F-BELV, the CITCA offices in Saigon failed to produce it. The report includes the following observation.

> It has been ascertained from the ICSC officials and other sources that aircraft F-BELV, chartered by the ICSC and missing during its flight from VIENTIANE to HANOI on 18 October 1965, was airworthy and a certificate of airworthiness for aircraft F-BELV is held by the CITCA offices in Saigon.

This seems an astonishing fact to accept as a given without any member of the ad-hoc committee having actually seen it, especially when they asked to have sight of it on two separate occasions, one of which was on a visit to the CITCA offices in Saigon by the committee's chairman, who spoke directly with the company's manager. Yet unnamed sources and unnamed ICSC officials tell them that the certificate of airworthiness is held at the CITCA offices in Saigon, and it appears to have been accepted without question. I am not suggesting that wasn't the case, but this report was an extremely important document and the question has to be asked, why didn't the members of the ad-hoc committee push the point and insist on seeing the document themselves? Moreover, if it was held at the Saigon office of CITCA, why could it not have been shown to the chairman of the committee when he visited that same office in Saigon? Finally, it is unsatisfactory to be so vague in such a report, the officials who were spoken to at the ICSC in Saigon should be named in the report, as should the names of the other 'sources' who confirmed the existence of the certificate of airworthiness. This report should never have been accepted without the missing names having been included.

The report also included a section on the searches that were carried out soon after the disappearance of F-BELV, this is covered in Chapter 11. Section (21) of the report talks about the likelihood of finding any survivors. This is interesting, as no allowance is made for the possibility of there being any survivors or, at best, the idea is quickly dismissed. The possibility that the aircraft may have landed somewhere and those on board taken prisoner, is also not considered as even a remote chance, and although it must be accepted that this is a highly unlikely probability, it should still have been considered.

This is what was said in the report:

> A greater portion of the terrain over which the courier plane flies is highly mountainous and it is covered with thick rainforests and very high trees. This mountainous and wooded area is very thinly populated, full of steep ravines with very few tracks. Wild animals as well as venomous snakes abound in this part of the country. On account of the rugged and inaccessible nature of the terrain, ground searches operations could not be carried out in Laos. Due to the extremely heavy foliage of the trees and thick jungle growth, even a low level aerial search did not help in locating the wreckage of the missing aircraft.

The report produced by Mr H.G. Hardy, and published on 11 January 1996, which was updated in January 2002, includes a slightly different version. It doesn't say that ground search operations in Laos 'could not be carried out', because of the rugged and inaccessible nature of the terrain. Instead it says, 'It is not known to what extent ground searches were conducted in Laos by the forces of the Royal Laotian Government, the Pathet Lao or the North Vietnamese.' This is a significant difference and is certainly something which needs clarification.

James took full advantage of his posting in Saigon, as it allowed him to sample the skills of the local tailors. A receipt dated 20 July 1965, from a tailor who catered for both civilian clothing and military uniforms, is contained within his service record. The receipt shows that he had trousers, a suit, shirts, dresses, army shirts, and women's blouses made. When James Byrne had his personal belongings collected from his room in Saigon, he still had some presents which he was either intending to send back home to his wife or take them back home with him on his next leave. These included: Vietnamese dolls; a Sampan model boat; a quantity of black material for making clothes; a silver pendant; a brooch; a chain; two pairs of high-heeled shoes, one red pair and one black; one pair of red-and-gold coloured women's slippers; one green silk dress and another that was purple-and-white in colour; two wicker handbags and two Coolie hats.

James' army service record included a Department of National Defence form, which was headed, 'Regular Forces Death Benefit Account'. On 21 April 1966, six months after the disappearance of flight F-BELV, and just three days after a Certificate of Presumption of Death had been issued officially determining him as deceased, his widow, Mrs Shelia E. Byrne, who was living in Aylmer, Quebec at the time, received a cheque for $3,000.00 under the terms of the Public Service Superannuation Act for a serving member of the Canadian armed forces. At the time, a similar sum of money would have purchased a three-bedroom terraced house in the United Kingdom. It was good to see that Canada looked after one of its 'adopted sons' in such a way.

A further payment that was sent to the Byrne family came from the Canadian Embassy in Paris, apparently from the owners of the aircraft F-BELV. In connection with this, a letter was received by Major A.F. Rippon, the Director of Personnel, and the Chief of the Defence Staff at the Canadian Forces Headquarters, in Elgin Street, Ottawa. It was headed:

Insurance Settlement – Byrne and Perkin

Further to our letter of June 28 we are pleased to inform you that our Embassy in Paris has received and transmitted to us a cheque from 'Les Experts Reunis' as the insurance settlement for the Byrne family. In accordance with the method of transmitting the payment suggested in your letter of February 23 we have attached a Canadian Government cheque for the sum of $17, 718.23 (CDN) payable to Mrs Sheila Byrne, and we would be grateful if you would ensure its transmission to Mrs Byrne.

We have received the settlement of the Perkin claim which we will forward as soon as the requisitioning of the cheque has been completed.

We would be grateful for confirmation the attached cheque has been transmitted to Mrs Byrne.

Signed
Under Secretary of State
For External Affairs.

The following letter was dated 2 May 1966, and was sent from Vice-Admiral K.L. Dyer, Chief of Personnel, at the Canadian Forces

Headquarters in Ottawa, to Mrs Sheila Byrne at her home address in Aylmer.

Dear Mrs Byrne,

It is with deep regret that, for official purposes, it must now be presumed that your husband, Sergeant James Sylvester Byrne, CD, died on 18 October 1965, the date on which he was first reported missing.

On behalf of the Minister of National Defence, the Defence Council and all personnel of the Canadian Forces, I extend heartfelt sympathy to you and your family in this sad bereavement.

Conclusion

As might be expected under the circumstances, there is no definitive answer regarding the fate of flight F-BELV. All we can do is look at the available facts taking into account all possible variables and then surmise what may have happened.

Fact number one: When flight F-BELV departed Vientiane it was in good mechanical condition, never having previously required any major mechanical overhaul to its engines or other mechanical parts.

Fact number two: The crew were all experienced airmen and Captain Domerque had flown the route, both ways, on many previous occasions. So, in regard to the journey, nothing would have come as a shock or surprise to him.

Fact number three: Flight F-BELV was last heard of at 1520 hours on Monday, 18 October 1965, fifteen minutes after it had departed Vientiane, when the aircraft's Captain, Henri Domerque, made radio contact with the North Vietnamese authorities at Gia Lam Airport, in Hanoi, to inform them that his estimated time of arrival was at 1658 hours later that same day.

Fact number four: Flight F-BELV never made it to Hanoi.

Fact number five: With no sight of or contact from any of the passengers or crew who were on board flight F-BELV, it can be safely assumed, with a fair degree of certainty, that after fifty-four years they are all now deceased.

None of the following details have been confirmed and are only conjecture and opinion as to what could have happened to flight F-BELV.

CONCLUSION

As I see it, there are three obvious possibilities, and a fourth option which is highly unlikely, but it still has to be included as a possible and feasible outcome. The first possibility is that there was catastrophic engine failure leading to total loss of power, causing the aircraft to crash. Secondly, the captain misjudged the height at which his aircraft was flying, hitting either the treetops or a hillside before crashing, killing everyone on board. The third possibility is that it was shot down by another aircraft or by ground fire. The fourth possibility, and admittedly the most unlikely of them all, is that flight F-BELV actually landed at Gia Lam Airport, and on arrival the crew and passengers were arrested and detained by the North Vietnamese, interrogated for information under the belief that one or more of those on board was involved in espionage, before been either killed or imprisoned.

Let us now take a look at what was taking place on the ground in Laos and North Vietnam at the time of flight F-BELV's disappearance. North and South Vietnam where in the midst of battle with each other, with similar conflict in Laos at the same time. On the day of the flight, in Laos, there was fighting both on the ground and in the air. Forces of the Royal Laotian Government were in conflict with forces of the communist-backed Pathet Lao. It is also known that there were anti-aircraft units operating in the area at that time.

I do not believe that flight F-BELV was lost due to flying at too low an altitude, before striking treetops or crashing into a hillside, this is for two reasons. The first reason being that there was good weather along the entire corridor of the flight path and, the second reason, the crew, especially the pilot, were experienced airmen on a flight which they had previously undertaken on numerous occasions.

I don't believe that flight F-BELV had a catastrophic engine failure which caused it to fall out of the sky, as there would still have been ample time for a 'May Day' message to be sent out by a crew member. This didn't happen, but if such a message was sent, it's strange that no one, from either side of the conflict, heard it.

I am therefore left with no alternative but to believe that flight F-BELV was either brought down by ground fire or from another aircraft, but as touched on in Chapter 5, it was more than likely the S-125 Neva, a Soviet made surface-to-air missile. I rule out the option of a collision with another aircraft due to the fact that there were no other reports of missing aircraft in the same area on the same day. As to the reason why it was shot down, that is a totally different question. There is no way that flight F-BELV could have been mistaken for a military aircraft, in fact all concerned parties on the ground would have been aware of the flight, and even if the two-hour time-delay for its departure from Vientiane is factored in, that should have made no difference as it was not a military aircraft, nor did it look like one.

Maybe the story of the mysterious American who met Donald J. Byrne, passing on information about James Sylvester Byrne being involved in intelligence work, has some substance to it as the reason why the flight was brought down by the North Vietnamese.

During the compilation of this book I have contacted: the Indian and Polish embassies in Hanoi, Vietnam; the Canadian Embassy in both Hanoi and Laos (which is actually in Bangkok, Thailand); the American National Archives; the French National Archives, and the Department for Foreign Affairs and International Trade. In relation to Compagnie Internationale de Transports Civil Aériens, the company who owned the F-BELV, I have been unable to find any trace of them still operating as a going concern. I also belatedly wrote a letter to the Chief of the Joint Staff in Ottawa:

Dear Sir,
On 18 October 1965, an International Commission of Supervision and Control aircraft disappeared on a flight from Saigon to Hanoi, somewhere between Laos and North Vietnam. Three of those on board the aircraft were

Canadians, one of them being Canadian Army Sergeant James Sylvester Byrne. He was my uncle, my mother's brother.

I am aware of the 'Pardy' report on the disappearance of the aircraft, flight F-BELV, which was produced in 1996 and updated in 2002. Since the latter of these dates, have there been any further updates on the matter?

As the aircraft has been missing now for some 54 years, are you in a position to confirm or deny whether James Sylvester Byrne was acting in an intelligence capacity, and that any such intelligence which he gathered was shared with the United States authorities. I ask as I am currently writing a book about the disappearance of flight F-BELV, and am exploring all possibilities and reasons as to how and why it went missing.

Despite all of these attempts to illicit further information in relation to the disappearance of F-BELV, none of them ever replied to my correspondence. Sadly, the mystery of the disappearance of the ICSC flight, F-BELV, remains a mystery.

In a strange way I felt slightly ill at ease asking those questions, but then I wouldn't be doing my job properly if I didn't. All I want to do is to find out what happened to F-BELV, see the aircraft located and for the bodies of those who perished to be recovered and given a proper burial. If that isn't possible, due to every avenue having been explored and exhausted, then that's fine, I can live with that, but if the whole story hasn't been told because individuals or governments aren't prepared to tell the entire truth about what they know of the disappearance of flight F-BELV, then that just isn't good enough. It is fifty-four years since the aircraft vanished and the families of those who perished have a right to know what happened to their loved ones, and why.

Sources

Primary Sources

Harbury, Jennifer K., *Truth, Torture, and the American Way: The History and Consequences of U.S. Involvement in Torture* (Beacon Press, 2005)
Robbins, Christopher, *Air America* (Macmillan, 1979)

Online Sources

Wikipedia
www.britishnewspaperarchive.co.uk
www.cia.gov
www.gendisasters.com
www.globalsecurity.org
www.history.com
www.thoughtco.com

About the Author

Stephen is a happily retired police officer having served with Essex Police as a constable for thirty years between 1983 and 2013. He is married to Tanya who is also his best friend.

Both his sons, Luke and Ross, were members of the armed forces, collectively serving five tours of Afghanistan between 2008 and 2013. Both were injured on their first tour. This led to Stephen's first book; *Two Sons in a Warzone – Afghanistan: The True Story of a Father's Conflict*, which was published in October 2010.

Both of his grandfathers served in and survived the First World War, one with the Royal Irish Rifles, the other in the Mercantile Navy, whilst his father was a member of the Royal Army Ordnance Corps during the Second World War.

Stephen collaborated with one of his writing partners, Ken Porter, on a previous book published in August 2012, *German P.O.W Camp 266: Langdon Hills*, which spent six weeks as the number one best-selling book in Waterstones, Basildon between March and April 2013. Steve and Ken collaborated on a further four books in the 'Towns & Cities in the Great War' series by Pen and Sword. Stephen has also written other titles in the same series of books, and in February 2017 his book *The Surrender of Singapore: Three Years of Hell 1942-45* was published. This was followed in March 2018 by *Against All Odds: Walter Tull the Black Lieutenant*, and in January 2019, *A History of The Royal Hospital Chelsea 1682–2017: The Warriors' Repose*, which he wrote with his wife, Tanya.

Stephen has also co-written three crime thrillers which were published between 2010 and 2012, which centre round a fictional Detective, named Terry Danvers.

When not writing, Tanya and he enjoy the simplicity of walking their three German shepherd dogs early each morning, at a time when most sensible people are still fast asleep in their beds.

Index